JUDY SCHULTZ

The Best of Seasons

RED DEER COLLEGE
PRESS

THE PUBLISHERS
Red Deer College Press
56 Avenue & 32 Street Box 5005
Red Deer Alberta Canada T4N 5H5

CREDITS
Designed by Robert MacDonald MediaClones Inc.
Toronto Ontario and Banff Alberta
Author photo by Steve Makris
Printed and bound in Canada by Commercial Colour Press
for Red Deer College Press

ACKNOWLEDGEMENTS
The publishers gratefully acknowledge the financial contribution of
The *Edmonton Journal* and Radio 7 CKRD. Special thanks to Nicole Markotic
and Patricia Roy for their generous assistance in
the preparation of this book.

Canadian Cataloguing in Publication Data

Shultz, Judy, 1943-
The best of seasons
ISBN 0-88995-049-0
1. Cookery I. Title
TX715.S38 1989 641.5 C89-091449-4

A Note about Sources

Every issue of The *Edmonton Journal* Food Section renews my gratitude to the multitude of good cooks who make up our sources–wire service test kitchens, favorite chefs and our own readers who have generously shared the best of their kitchens during our annual recipe contests. I have attempted to attribute sources whenever possible.

And thank you to Gordon Morash, who minded the store for me while this book was coming together; to Shelagh Robinson, who sat faithfully over a hot computer until the last word had been entered; and to our photographers, Dan Jurak and Steve Makris, whose sensitive and beautiful food art appears in this book.

A Note to Readers

Both imperial and metric measures have been included in recipes throughout this book. Because it is not possible to convert exactly, the two systems have been balanced separately, and readers are reminded not to use a combination of both systems of measures in their preparation of recipes.

Contents

Introduction

For the past eight years, the focus of my week has been Tuesday, the day we put The *Edmonton Journal's* Food Section together.

When I was asked to develop the Food Section, I decided I would fill our pages with perfect things to eat, lovingly prepared the way my own family did it–no short cuts, no add-water-and-stir convenience foods, none of what my mother called "cheap tricks."

But that was a while ago, and in the meantime a generation of women who would traditionally have been at home cooking those perfect meals have gone into the workforce. The ones who remain at home are busier than ever. Cooks of both sexes have developed more eclectic tastes and a newly awakened interest in nutrition and the environment. And, above all, they have less time for scratch cooking.

That's why you will find convenience items in some of these recipes, plus a few ingredients your mother never heard of. It's also the reason for the "Fast Track" section at the end of each chapter.

Food is not only *one* of the great universal pleasures, it is also the *essential* pleasure. For me, it's more than that–it's a passion. I love the way it looks and tastes and smells.

Wherever I travel, I meet people who share this passion.

I meet them in their kitchens, their restaurants and vineyards, their markets and even their fishing boats. I hear about their lives, and sometimes we share a meal. And after that, we understand each other a little better.

I hope you'll find this book to be the way food should always be–simple, welcome and comforting. *Bon appétit.*

Judy Schultz
Edmonton July 1989

CHAPTER 1
January

Nouveau Riches

January Recipes

There was a time when fruit meant apples and cheese meant Cheddar, and nobody in North America had ever heard of a kiwi.

Except for bananas and the odd yam, tropical produce was rare in this neck of the woods. Did it matter to grandma that there were hundreds of different mangoes dropping off trees in Asia? And if some of them smelled of jasmine and spice while others reeked subtley of *eau de turpentine*, did she care?

She did not. Mangoes were for travel posters. Here, in the real world, she had other problems, like how to keep her potatoes from freezing during winter.

That, as they say, is history. The food business is one of continual change and frequent astonishment, and I never enjoy it more than in January, when I burrow through the drifts and leap joyously into my favorite produce market. The whole place glows with the latest fashion in food. Mangoes, papayas, jicama, chayote, sapotas, kiwanos, breadfruit, carambola…carambola?

Several years ago I found a yellow-green, star-shaped fruit in a market in Chinatown. It was just about the prettiest thing I'd ever seen.

"Carambola," said the man in the apron. "Special price today."

So I bought four caram-whatevers and carted them back to my kitchen. I sliced the big one in half and stared at it for a while before I started chewing. It was hard, sour and dry, and made my teeth feel furry.

Undaunted, I tackled the smallest one next. When in doubt, fry, so it went into the pan with some butter and a little fresh ginger. Stir-fried, it wasn't bad. But it wasn't good either.

I decided to think about the other two for a while, so number three and four sat in a fruit bowl looking elegant until one of them shriveled and the other grew fur. So much for carambola, I thought. Next time I'll buy some nice plastic fruit.

As it happened, the next carambolas showed up in a welcome-to-Hong Kong fruit bowl that came with my hotel room one humid night. "Ha, plastic fruit," I thought, and fell into bed. But at 4 am, wide awake and hungry enough to eat a horse, I dug into the only edible thing in the room: carambola. It was that or the orchids. Surprise! This time the flesh was sweet, juicy and almost citrus in flavor. Delicious. I ate two. The difference was subtle, but important–these ones were ripe.

Now I have a couple of questions for the produce people. Why didn't somebody tell me the first ones were green enough to choke a goat? And where is it written that quince, which is horrible in its raw state, (yes, I tried one), will be meltingly soft and sweet once you've baked it with a dash of cinnamon? Who tells us that cooking endive in a cast-iron pan will turn its creamy flesh battleship gray? Certainly not the pink-cheeked kid in the long apron, slamming tomatoes onto a pile. What we need is a good set of instructions, like the ones that come with Lego: "Peel part 1, Steam part 2, Eat part 3," and so forth.

In this chapter, we look at fashions in food and what to do with them, not just because they're trendy, but because they represent a larger world of tastes and textures. Grandma would have loved it.

Marinated Chevre

There's nothing like marinated goat cheese for flavor, especially with a glass of wine. I like to use an Italian oil with this, preferably Tuscan, because of the wonderfully nutty flavor. If you can't find fresh sage leaves, use 1/2 tsp (2 mL) dry sage instead.

6 oz	small chevre	168 g
	extra virgin olive oil	
5 or 6	garlic cloves	5 or 6
2 or 3	sage leaves	2 or 3
10	brine-cured black olives	10

Put cheese in a glass dish that is just big enough to hold it. Cover cheese with oil. Peel and slightly crush garlic and add it along with sage leaves and olives. Cover and refrigerate 2 or 3 days before serving with sliced baguette or sourdough bread. Serve marinating oil on the side so guests can drizzle it over bread. If there is oil left over, it will be excellent in a salad or over cooked vegetables. Serves 4 as an appetizer.

Crisp Chayote Strips

The Incas and the Aztecs grew chayote, which is a mild, crisp squash that takes well to deep-frying.

2	chayotes	2
1/3 cup	flour	75 mL
1	egg	1
1 tbsp	milk	15 mL
1 cup	cornflakes, finely crushed	250 mL
1/3 cup	vegetable oil	75 mL
	salt	
	hot salsa	

Peel chayotes, cut into halves and remove large middle seeds. Slice chayotes into thin strips. Roll in flour. Beat egg and milk together in a medium bowl. Dip floured chayote strips in egg mixture, then in cornflakes. Heat oil in a large skillet. Add strips a few at a time and fry until golden brown, about 3 minutes. Drain on paper towels. Sprinkle with salt. Serve hot, in a napkin-lined basket, with a hot salsa for dipping. A great snack with cold beer. Serves 4.

Pistachio Pasta

Have you ever wondered why pistachios are dyed bright pink (or sometimes chalky white)? The shells sometimes blemish without affecting the nut, and the dye hides the blemish. That handy bit of trivia, and this recipe, came to me from the California Pistachio Board.

1	clove garlic, minced	1
1/4 cup	onion, chopped	50 mL
2 tbsp	olive oil	30 mL
1/2 cup	shelled pistachios, coarsely chopped	125 mL
1/4 cup	ripe olives, chopped	50 mL
1/4 cup	fresh parsley, minced	50 mL
1 tsp	lemon juice	5 mL
5 or 6	fresh basil leaves, minced	5 or 6
8 oz	spaghetti, cooked and drained	224 g
1/3 cup	Parmesan cheese, grated	75 mL
	pepper to taste	

Sauté garlic and onion in olive oil until tender. Add pistachios, olives, parsley, lemon juice, pepper, basil and spaghetti, tossing together to blend thoroughly. Toss with Parmesan and serve immediately. Serves 4 to 6.

Eggplant Caviar

There are so many recipes for eggplant caviar that one more can't hurt. This one, which is less garlicy than most, came from Theo, a Greek friend, who uses it as a cold pasta sauce.

2	small eggplants	2
4 tbsp	fresh lemon juice	60 mL
4 tbsp	olive oil	60 mL
1	large clove garlic	1
1/4 tsp	paprika	1 mL
1/2 tsp	cayenne	2 mL
2	green onions, finely minced	2
1	tomato, seeded and chopped	1
1/2 cup	fresh parsley, chopped	125 mL
1 tsp	salt	5 mL
1/2 tsp	pepper, freshly ground	2 mL

Preheat oven to 400 F (200 C). Pierce eggplant in several places. Bake in preheated oven about 30 minutes, or until very soft. Split eggplant open and scoop out pulp. In a blender, place eggplant pulp, lemon juice, olive oil, garlic, paprika and cayenne. Blend until smooth and light. Stir in green onions, tomato and parsley. Season with salt and freshly ground pepper. Serve with warm pita bread or melba toast. Serves 4 as an appetizer.

Pico di Gallo

Jicama, a brown-skinned root vegetable with crisp, mild flesh, comes from Mexico and Central America. It is eaten raw in this salad.

4 cups	raw jicama, diced	1 L
1	stalk celery, diced	1
1	jalapeño pepper, seeded and minced	1
2 cups	orange segments	500 mL
1 tsp	lime peel, grated	5 mL
2 tbsp	fresh lime juice	30 mL
2 tsp	sugar	10 mL
1 tsp	salt	5 mL

Combine all ingredients in a glass bowl and marinate at least 1 hour. To serve, mound on a platter and garnish with slices of orange and lime. Serves 6.

Fennel and Bean Salad with Garlic Dressing

This recipe was inspired by Lilliana, a cook who fed me well during one summer in Tuscany. She served it with fried rabbit, but it's just as good with cold ham or chicken.

DRESSING

1/3 cup	red wine vinegar	75 mL
1/4 cup	olive oil	50 mL
1	garlic clove, minced	1
2 tsp	fresh oregano **OR**	10 mL
1 tsp	dried oregano	5 mL
1/4 cup	fresh parsley, minced	50 mL
1/4 tsp	each, freshly ground black pepper, fennel seeds and salt	1 mL

Put all ingredients into a jar with a tight-fitting lid. Shake to blend. Reserve.

SALAD

1 lb	fresh green beans, trimmed and cut	500 g
1	large fennel bulb	1
2 cups	canned chick peas, drained	500 mL
1	small sweet red pepper, sliced	1
1	stalk celery, diced	1

Cook green beans in boiling water until tender-crisp, about 10 minutes. Drain, rinse under cold water and put in a salad bowl.

Cut top from fennel bulb, reserving a few feathery fronds for garnish. Peel away any brown or damaged outer leaves and chop coarsely. You should have about 1 1/2 cups (375 mL). Add fennel to green beans.

Add chick peas, sweet red pepper and celery. Pour dressing over salad. Toss to mix. Cover with plastic wrap and refrigerate about 1 hour. Garnish with fennel fronds. Serves 4 to 6.

Wild Rice Salad with Squash

This is the salad to serve with duck or grilled chicken. Use the youngest squash you can find and, if you wish, substitute brown or white rice for part (or all) of the wild rice.

SALAD

4 cups	cooked wild rice	1 L
4	small yellow squash (round or crookneck)	4
4	small green squash (patty or zucchini)	4

DRESSING

3/4 cup	pistachio nuts, shelled	175 mL
2 tsp	fresh tarragon, chopped **OR**	10 mL
1 tsp	dried tarragon	5 mL
1/2 tsp	dried sage	2 mL
1	green onion, chopped	1
3 tbsp	rice wine vinegar	45 mL
1 tbsp	Dijon mustard	15 mL
2 tsp	honey	10 mL
3 tbsp	vegetable oil	45 mL
1/2 tsp	white pepper	2 mL

Wash and thinly slice squash. Arrange in a fan pattern around 4 plates. In a small bowl whisk together all dressing ingredients, then toss with rice and spoon mixture over squash. Serves 4.

Note: Pine nuts or slivered, toasted almonds may be substituted for pistachio nuts.

Samuel Twining's Savory Rice

An unusual use for this fragrant tea.

2 tbsp	butter	30 mL
1	onion, diced	1
1 cup	long grain rice	250 mL
1 tsp	turmeric	5 mL
1 tsp	mixed herbs	5 mL
2 cups	Twinings Earl Grey tea, brewed	500 mL
1/2 tsp	salt	2 mL

Melt butter in a pan, and sauté onions and rice about 5 minutes. Add turmeric and herbs. Stir well. Add tea and salt, cover the pan and steam on lowest heat possible, about 30 minutes, or until rice is cooked but still slightly firm. Serves 4.

Salmon with Star Fruit

4	salmon steaks, 1 inch (2 cm) thick	4
	salt and pepper to taste	
2 tbsp	mayonnaise	30 mL
1 tbsp	soya sauce	15 mL
1/2 cup	water	125 mL
1	large star fruit, sliced (do not peel)	1
1/4 cup	fresh parsley, chopped	50 mL
2	lemons, cut into wedges	2

Preheat oven to 400 F (200 C). If fish is frozen, thaw. Wipe fish with a damp towel and place in a buttered baking dish. Season with salt and pepper. Mix mayonnaise, soya sauce and water. Pour over fish. Place in the preheated oven 8 minutes.

Add sliced star fruit and continue baking 6 minutes longer.

Remove fish to a platter. Arrange sliced star fruit on and around fish. Drizzle with pan juices. Sprinkle with parsley and serve with lemon wedges. Serves 4.

Spicy Peanut Chicken

Thai food has become so popular that it's hard to keep peanut butter in stock these days. This spicy Thai dish was a winner in one of The *Edmonton Journal's* recipe contests. Serve with rice or noodles.

2/3 cup	flour	150 mL
	salt and pepper to taste	
1/4 tsp	oregano	1 mL
1/4 tsp	cayenne	1 mL
2 tsp	paprika	10 mL
3 lbs	chicken, cut up	1.5 kg
2 tbsp	oil	30 mL
2 cups	mushrooms, sliced	500 mL
2 tbsp	onion, finely chopped	30 mL
2 tbsp	butter	30 mL
1/4 cup	orange juice concentrate	50 mL
1/3 cup	peanut butter	75 mL
2 tsp	dried red peppers, crushed	10 mL
1/2 tsp	chili powder	2 mL
1 cup	chicken broth	250 mL
	cilantro leaves to garnish	

Preheat oven to 325 F (160 C). Combine flour, salt, black pepper, oregano, cayenne and paprika in a plastic bag. Wash chicken well and pull off excess fat. Shake each piece in the bag until coated with flour mixture. Heat oil in a large frypan. Brown chicken on all sides and lay pieces in a 9 inch (2 L) baking dish.

Cook mushrooms and onion in butter over medium-high heat until onion is just transparent. With a slotted spoon, remove vegetables and reserve. To pan juices, add orange juice concentrate and peanut butter, stirring well to mix. Add remaining spices and chicken broth. Bring to simmer and remove from heat. Add cooked mushrooms and onions to sauce. Spoon over chicken pieces.

Cover and bake 45 minutes. Remove cover and continue baking 15 minutes longer. Garnish with cilantro leaves. Serves 4 to 6.

Papaya Seed Dressing

Use this papaya seed dressing for a salad of avocado, orange and grapefruit, or drizzle it over avocado slices.

2 tbsp	papaya seeds	30 mL
2 tbsp	honey	30 mL
4 tbsp	lemon juice	60 mL
1/2 cup	salad oil	125 mL
pinch	salt	pinch

Place all ingredients in a blender and process until seeds are chopped. Makes about 1 cup (250 mL).

Quince Crisp

The quince looks like a pear that didn't quite make it–yellow, oddly shaped and hard and sour in its raw state. But when cooked with honey or sugar, it becomes fragrant and utterly delicious.

4	quinces	4
	juice of 1 lemon	
1 tsp	lemon rind, grated	5 mL
1/4 cup	sugar	50 mL
1 tsp	cinnamon	5 mL
1/4 cup	water	50 mL
3 tbsp	butter	45 mL
1/2 cup	quick rolled oats	125 mL
1/2 cup	brown sugar	125 mL

Preheat oven to 375 F (190 C). Peel, core and slice quinces. Lay in a buttered 1 qt (1 L) casserole and sprinkle with lemon juice. Stir lemon rind, sugar and cinnamon together, and toss with fruit slices. Add water.

Cut butter into oats and brown sugar until crumbly. Sprinkle evenly over sliced quinces. Bake, uncovered, about 30 minutes. Serve warm, with lightly sweetened yogurt. Serves 4.

FAST TRACK MENU

Shrimp with Ginger and Chili Sauce
Mango with Rum and Lime

When you have to cook on the fast track, there's no time to waste cleaning shrimp. Buy it deveined, either fresh or frozen. Boil a pot of water and make those Fast Track reliables–pasta or rice. If you're cutting calories, try serving with steamed spaghetti squash, steamed bean sprouts or iceberg lettuce sliced into thin julienne.

Shrimp with Ginger and Chili Sauce

This was another winner in The *Edmonton Journal's* Favorite Recipes Contest. After you taste it, you'll know why.

2 1/2 lb	medium raw shrimps, cleaned	1.25 kg
4 tbsp	vegetable oil	60 mL
2	scallions, chopped	2
2	cloves garlic, finely minced	2
1/2 inch	slice fresh ginger root, peeled and finely minced	2 cm
1 tsp	hot chili sauce (from Oriental specialty stores)	5 mL
2 tsp	rice wine (sake) or dry sherry	10 mL
1	small onion, sliced	1
2 tbsp	sugar	30 mL
2 tbsp	ketchup	30 mL
2 tsp	soya sauce	10 mL

Heat oil in a wok or skillet until almost smoking. Toss in scallions, garlic and ginger. Stir-fry 30 seconds, then add shrimp, chili sauce and wine. Reduce heat slightly and stir-fry until shrimps are pink.

Add onion. Stir-fry 2 minutes, then add sugar, ketchup and soya sauce. Continue stir-frying until sauce is thick and clings to onions and shrimp, about 2 minutes. Serves 4.

Mango with Rum and Lime

A ripe mango is one of the most decadent pleasures this side of Eden.

2	large ripe mangoes	2
2 tbsp	butter	30 mL
2 tbsp	brown sugar	30 mL
2 tbsp	lime or lemon juice	30 mL
3 tbsp	orange liqueur	45 mL
3 tbsp	rum	45 mL
4	large scoops vanilla ice cream	4
	slice of lime or lemon	

Halve and peel mangoes. Cut each half in 4 or 5 long slices.

Heat butter in a heavy frypan over moderate heat. Add brown sugar and lime juice, and stir briefly. Add mango slices. Shake the pan gently until fruit has softened and plumped up a bit, usually about 3 minutes, depending on ripeness.

Add liqueur and rum. Using a long match, light liquids. Shake the pan until flame dies. Immediately divide mixture onto dessert plates. Put a scoop of ice cream on each and serve at once, garnished with lime. Serves 4.

CHAPTER 2
February

Comfort Me With...

February Recipes

When February has us by the scruff of our collective necks, a touch of comfort is in order.

"Comfort me with apples, for I am sick of love," cried the poet, which is all very well if you're another poet, or it's the middle of September. But in February I wish for softer, warmer dishes. Snuggly food.

Rice pudding with fat raisins and nutmeg. Bean soup. Real hot chocolate. Bread and gravy–now there's a comforter.

One of the best friends I ever had was a bread and gravy specialist. She was a cookie-baking, music-making, tea-brewing woman who never bothered to marry because she could never find the time.

In February her tiny, crowded house became a fortress at one end of the longest, coldest three-block street in Saskatchewan. It was my street, and I was the kid who lived at the other end.

I liked to drop in on winter Sundays. She'd let my dog sit on the furniture, and she didn't believe in letting her guests go hungry, especially in cold weather.

In the biggest chair imaginable we would thaw out, dog and child, aiming our feet at the leaping flames in her wood-burning stove while she revived us with hot, sweet tea and oatmeal cookies.

The bread and gravy came later, when it was nearly dark and the storm was still roaring.

By that time she would have checked the window.

"I can't see the doctor's house anymore. Not fit for man or beast out there," she'd say, grinning at my dog. He'd grin back and start licking the cookie crumbs off his paws so he'd be neat for supper.

About five o'clock she'd take the cast-iron frypan off its wall-nail and start frying an onion. Wisely, she started most winter meals with a fried onion; it gave her time to consider the infinite possibilities that lay ahead–mushroom soup on toast, curried bananas on peanut-buttered toast (exotic stuff, that), creamed asparagus on toast.

But when it was the day after roast beef, we didn't do toast; those were strictly bread and gravy days.

The gravy started out cold and stiff and hopeless looking, having reposed all that February day in the back porch window. I'd watch, fascinated, as that rubbery blob melted into a dark, glossy, aromatic puddle, and she'd stir furiously while it bubbled and fumed, smelling better than the original roast ever could have.

Bread-and-gravy went like this: Thick slice of homemade bread. Big ladle of gravy with butter-browned onions. Speck of black pepper. Ketchup on the side for emergencies, which never arose.

I always felt better after bread and gravy, as though I could face the icy remains of winter and survive until spring.

Real Hot Chocolate

Here's the best comforter of all. It's made like this at the Maison du Chocolat in Paris for about $6 a cup.

3	squares unsweetened chocolate	3
1/2 cup	sugar	125 mL
1 cup	water	250 mL
3 cups	milk	750 mL
dash	salt	dash

Combine chocolate, sugar, salt and water in a medium saucepan. Cook over low heat, stirring constantly, 5 minutes, or until chocolate is melted. Stir in milk slowly and heat just until piping hot, but do not boil. Beat until foamy-topped. Serve with whipped cream if you wish. Serves 4.

Orange French Toast

When one of my favorite restaurants stopped serving this, I cried.

6	eggs	6
2	oranges	2
1/4 cup	milk	50 mL
1/4 cup	orange liqueur (optional)	50 mL
2 tbsp	granulated sugar	30 mL
1/4 tsp	vanilla	1 mL
1/4 tsp	salt	1 mL
8	slices French bread	8
1 cup	sour cream	250 mL
2 tbsp	brown sugar	30 mL
	icing sugar for garnish	
	oil for frying	

Preheat oven to 200 F (100 C). Finely grate the peel of one orange and set aside. Squeeze oranges–you need about 2/3 cup (150 mL) of juice.

Beat eggs in a large mixing bowl. Add juice of oranges, milk, orange liqueur, sugar, vanilla, salt and 1/2 grated orange peel. Dip each slice of bread in egg mixture, turning to coat both sides.

In a large lightly-greased skillet, fry bread on both sides. Keep warm in oven.

To make topping, combine sour cream, brown sugar and remaining orange peel in a small bowl. Chill in refrigerator until serving time.

Sprinkle toast with icing sugar and top with sour cream mixture. Serves 4.

Welsh Rarebit with Hot Salsa

On cold nights when you don't feel like cooking, or you think you're about to have a run-in with the flu, this is a definite comforter.

1 cup	beer	250 mL
1 tsp	dry mustard	5 mL
2 tsp	Worcestershire sauce	10 mL
dash	Tabasco sauce	dash
4 cups	Cheddar cheese, grated	1 L
2 tbsp	hot salsa	30 mL
2	eggs	2
8	slices toast	8

Combine beer, mustard, Worcestershire and Tabasco in top of a double boiler. Heat over simmering water. Gradually stir in cheese until melted. Stir in hot salsa.

Beat eggs slightly in a small bowl, then slowly stir in about 1 cup (250 mL) hot cheese mixture; return to double boiler. Cook, stirring, 3 minutes.

Halve each slice of toast diagonally; place 4 triangles on each serving plate and spoon cheese mixture over top. Serves 4.

Hootsla

This is real comfort food. Terrific for morning, but just as good at midnight if you're so inclined.

2 tbsp	butter	30 mL
2	slices stale bread, cubed	2
1	green onion, minced	1
2	eggs, beaten	2
	salt and pepper to taste	

Melt butter in a small frypan. Add bread and onion, and cook until barely browned. Add eggs and stir briefly, removing from heat almost at once because eggs set quickly. If you're in the mood for cheese, you might like to grate some over top while it's still hot. Serves 1.

Tuscan Bean Soup

Every cook in Tuscany has a different version of bean soup, but I'm partial to this one, especially in winter. Serve it with fresh, warm bread and green onions. And a bottle of chianti can't hurt.

1 cup	dried white beans	250 mL
1/2 cup	dried kidney beans	125 mL
1	onion, stuck with 3 cloves	1
1	stalk celery, chopped	1
1	bay leaf	1
1 tbsp	olive oil	15 mL
2 tsp	butter	10 mL
2	large onions, chopped	2
1	carrot, chopped	1
4	slices Prosciutto ham, chopped	4
1	dried hot chili, crumbled	1
28 oz	can plum tomatoes	875 g
1	green pepper, chopped	1
1 tsp	dried oregano	5 mL
	fresh parsley, chopped, for garnish	
	olive oil	
	Parmesan cheese	
	salt to taste	

Cover beans with cold water. Soak overnight and drain.

In a Dutch oven, cover beans with 6 cups cold water. Add celery, onion and bay leaf. Bring to boil. Reduce heat and simmer, covered, until beans are tender. Drain beans and discard celery, onion and bay leaf. Reserve 1/2 cup (125 mL) beans for thickening.

Add oil and butter to beans over medium heat. Add chopped onions, carrot, ham and crumbled pepper, and cook, stirring occasionally, about 5 minutes.

Add tomatoes, crushing them slightly. Add green pepper and oregano. Mash reserved beans and stir in.

Taste for seasoning and add salt if needed. Prop the lid halfway off so steam can escape. Simmer 45 minutes. Serve, adding parsley and a few drops of olive oil to each bowl. And pass around some Parmesan cheese. Serves 6 to 8.

Note: If you find this soup (or any soup) too thick for your taste, just add water.

Oyster Soup with Brie and Champagne

The food and wine snobs of this world tend to turn up their noses at those of us who love the bubbly. We see them subtly raise an eyebrow and twitch a lip when we suggest bollinger with breakfast. A pox on them, I say.

Of all the wines I love (and there are many), champagne is the one that comforts me most. You don't need a lot of it for this superbly rich soup, so there'll be some left to comfort the cook.

24	small oysters (save the juices)	24
1/2 cup	butter	125 mL
1/2 cup	onion, coarsely chopped	125 mL
1/2 cup	flour	125 mL
3 cups	water with oyster juice added	750 mL
1 lb	brie, peeled and diced	500 g
2 cups	whipping cream, at room temperature	500 mL
1 cup	champagne	250 mL
	salt and pepper to taste	

Shuck oysters, reserving juice, or use shucked raw oysters packed in juice.

Strain through a fine sieve to remove any gritty bits. Melt butter in a saucepan and sauté onions until translucent. Sprinkle in flour and whisk until mixture is smooth and bubbly. Slowly add water and oyster juices, whisking constantly to keep mixture smooth. Add cheese and keep whisking until melted, about 5 minutes. Return to the pot and bring to simmer. Stir in cream. As soon as soup simmers again, add champagne.

Remove the pot from the stove and add oysters. The heat of the soup will be sufficient to cook them. Season and ladle soup into bowls. Serves 8.

Freddie's Mussels

A big-hearted chef named Freddie Girard prepared these for 4 hungry women one cold night in Montréal when our car wouldn't start. And while we ate, he started the car. Freddie, wherever you are, we love ya!

5 dozen	mussels	5 dozen
1/4 cup	butter	50 mL
1/4 cup	shallots, finely chopped	50 mL
3	garlic cloves, minced	3
1 1/2 cups	dry white wine	375 mL
1	lemon	1
	pepper, freshly ground	
	fresh parsley, chopped	

Scrub mussels to remove sand. Pull off beards. Discard any mussels that are open.

Melt butter in a big pot. Add shallots and garlic. Fry until soft. Add wine. Bring to boil and immediately reduce heat to low simmer. Add cleaned mussels.

Cover kettle and simmer 5 to 6 minutes, or until mussels open. (Some may take a little longer.) Remove cooked mussels with a slotted spoon. Reserve mussels, discarding any that haven't opened.

Strain broth through a double thickness cheesecloth to remove grit. Serve with broth in individual shallow bowls with lemon wedges on the side. Just before serving, throw in a big handful of parsley. Serve with a basket of warm French bread for sopping up the juices. Beer or a dry white wine goes well here. Serves 4.

Baked Clams with Garlic

Steamed clams are simple and lovely, but these are even better, being intensely garlicy. Serve with good bread and beer or a cool bottle of dry white wine.

24	small clams on half-shell	24
1	fresh lemon	1
4 tbsp	butter	60 mL
4	garlic cloves, minced	4
1/2 cup	fresh parsley, chopped	125 mL
4	slices bacon, diced	4

Preheat oven to 425 F (220 C). Squeeze a few drops lemon juice over each clam and arrange on a cookie sheet. Melt butter in a saucepan, and add garlic and parsley. Divide mixture among clams. Sprinkle bacon over clams. Bake until sizzling, about 6 to 8 minutes. Serves 2 as a main course, 4 as an appetizer.

Pasta with Cream and Wild Mushrooms

Here's a simple, sensual dish for 2. Almost any wild mushroom will do, but Porcini are especially delicious. (Dried wild mushrooms are available at specialty counters and delis.)

2 oz	dried wild mushrooms	60 g
1 cup	fresh mushrooms, sliced	250 mL
3 tbsp	butter	45 mL
1	small onion, chopped	1
2	thin slices Prosciutto ham, shredded	2
1/2 cup	whipping cream	125 mL
1/4 cup	fresh parsley, chopped	50 mL
1/2 cup	Parmesan, grated	125 mL
	salt and pepper	
2 cups	fresh noodles	500 mL

Soak wild mushrooms about 10 minutes, in enough cold water to cover. Drain, squeeze dry and chop.

Melt 2 tbsp (30 mL) butter in a frypan. Add onion, ham and mushrooms. Cook about 5 minutes. Stir in cream and parsley, about 2 tsp (10 mL) cheese and a dash salt. Grind in pepper. Reduce heat and keep warm.

Cook noodles until tender. Drain. Add remaining butter and 1 tbsp (15 mL) cheese. Pour into a warm dish. Make a well in the center and pour in sauce. Pass around remaining cheese. Serves 2.

Creamy Whipped Potatoes

Jamin, a restaurant in Paris, has built its reputation on its whipped potatoes. I like these almost as much, and they can be frozen.

4 to 5	large potatoes	4 to 5
1 cup	2 percent cottage cheese	250 mL
1 cup	plain yogurt	250 mL
1	green onion, finely minced	1
2 tsp	butter	10 mL

Preheat oven to 350 F (180 C). Boil and mash potatoes. Whip cottage cheese in a blender or food processor until smooth. Add cheese, yogurt, onion and butter to mashed potatoes. Beat until creamy. Taste for seasoning, adding salt if necessary.

Turn into a buttered 1 qt (1 L) casserole dish. Dot with additional butter. Bake, covered, 35 minutes. Serves 6.

Sunday Chicken

A simple, fast chicken dish.

8	boneless chicken breasts	8
3/4 cup	buttermilk	175 mL
2 tsp	onion flakes	10 mL
1 1/2 cups	cracker crumbs, finely crushed	375 mL
1/3 cup	orange marmalade	75 mL
2 tbsp	lemon juice	30 mL
2 tsp	Dijon mustard	10 mL
1 tsp	chili powder	5 mL

Preheat oven to 350 F (180 C). Let onion flakes soak in buttermilk 1/2 an hour. Dip chicken in buttermilk and then in cracker crumbs. Place on a foil-lined cookie sheet. Bake 15 minutes.

Meanwhile, combine marmalade, lemon juice and mustard to make a glaze. Brush chicken with glaze and continue roasting another 30 minutes, or until no longer pink in the middle. Serves 8.

Chocolate Peanut Butter Fudge

There are times when the only real comfort is fudge. No matter what disaster has you by the throat–romance fizzled, job down the tube, somebody stole your Porsche–fudge will help. And this one is so easy you can't ruin it.

1 cup	peanut butter chips	250 mL
1 cup	semisweet chocolate chips	250 mL
2 1/4 cups	sugar	550 mL
1 3/4 cups	marshmallow creme	425 mL
3/4 cup	evaporated milk	175 mL
1/4 cup	butter	50 mL
1 tsp	vanilla	5 mL

Measure peanut butter chips into 1 mixing bowl and chocolate chips into another. Set aside. Butter a 9 inch (2 L) square pan and set aside.

Combine sugar, marshmallow creme, evaporated milk and butter in a 3 qt (3 L) saucepan. Cover over medium heat, stirring constantly until mixture boils. Continue cooking 5 minutes, stirring constantly.

Remove from heat. Stir in vanilla. Immediately stir 1/2 hot mixture into peanut butter chips until they melt completely. Pour into a prepared pan.

Stir remaining hot mixture into chocolate chips until completely melted. Spread over top of peanut butter layer. Cool and cut into 24 squares.

Rice Custard Pudding

Here's a pudding that will bring a nostalgic tear to the eye of anyone whose grandmother was a great cook.

3 cups	milk	750 mL
1 cup	whipping cream	250 mL
1/2 cup	uncooked long-grain rice	125 mL
1 cup	raisins	250 mL
3	eggs, separated	3
3/4 cup	sugar	175 mL
1/4 tsp	salt	1 mL
1 tsp	vanilla	5 mL
	nutmeg, freshly ground	

Preheat oven to 350 F (180 C). Combine milk and cream in a double boiler over simmering water. Stir in rice and cover. Cook, stirring occasionally to prevent sticking, until rice is tender and creamy and all liquid is absorbed, about 1 1/2 to 2 hours. Remove from heat.

Generously butter a deep 8 cup (2 L) glass or ceramic baking dish. Beat egg yolks in a large bowl until frothy. Beat in sugar, salt and vanilla. Gradually stir in hot rice and raisins.

Beat egg whites in a small bowl until soft peaks form. Fold into rice mixture. Turn mixture into the prepared baking dish. Sprinkle top with nutmeg. Place the baking dish in a shallow pan, then put the pan in the oven. Pour boiling water into the outer pan to a depth of 2 inches (5 cm).

Bake 45 minutes. Remove baking dish from water and allow pudding to cool to room temperature before serving. Serves 6.

FAST TRACK MENU

Vermicelli Aglio e Olio
Italian Stir-Fry
Sautéed Apples with Ice Cream

The vermicelli is a light but comforting dish for a winter night, and takes no more than 12 minutes, start to finish. The stir-fry will take slightly longer, but tastes perfect when you're ravenous.

Vermicelli Aglio e Olio

3	large cloves garlic, minced	3
1/2 cup	extra virgin olive oil	125 mL
1 lb	vermicelli	500 g
	Parmesan cheese to taste, freshly grated	
	pepper to taste	

Sauté garlic in olive oil 10 minutes. Do not brown. Cover and keep hot. Meanwhile, cook pasta in rapidly boiling salted water until barely *al dente*. Drain in colander, reserving 1/4 cup (50 mL) cooking water. Stir reserved water into garlic-oil mixture. Pour over vermicelli and toss. Serve with Parmesan and pass the pepper mill. Serves 4.

Italian Stir-Fry

This contest-winning recipe is a personal favorite. Serve it with pasta or bread.

4	hot Italian sausages	4
1 tbsp	olive oil	15 mL
1	medium onion, coarsely chopped	1
1	clove garlic, minced	1
1	small eggplant, cubed	1
4	small zucchini, thinly sliced	4
1	small green pepper, seeded, cut into strips	1
1	small red pepper, seeded, cut into strips	1
1/2 cup	tomato juice or water	125 mL
2	tomatoes, cut into wedges	2
	salt, pepper, oregano and Italian seasoning to taste	

Cut sausages into thin slices. In a large frypan brown sausages in oil. Remove from pan and set aside.

Add onion to the pan and cook until slightly softened. Add garlic and eggplant, cook, stirring, until slightly softened. Add zucchini and peppers, and continue to fry 2 to 3 minutes. Add tomato juice and browned sausages. Sprinkle lightly with salt, pepper, oregano and Italian seasoning.

Cover and allow to steam until nearly tender. Taste and adjust seasoning. Add tomatoes, cover and cook 1 to 2 minutes longer, or until vegetables are tender-crisp. Serves 4.

Sautéed Apples with Ice Cream

2	apples, peeled, cored and cut	2
2 tbsp	butter	30 mL
1/2 cup	sugar	125 mL

Melt butter in a frypan, add apples and sprinkle with sugar. Stir-fry over medium heat until transparent. Serve over vanilla or maple walnut ice cream. Serves 4.

CHAPTER 3
March

Help! Help!

March Recipes

There is a feeling among some foodies that any dish not requiring eight hours of shopping, fifteen exotic ingredients and three days' preparation is not worth putting on a plate.

Normally, I'm a scratch cook myself. God knows, I love the smell of bubbling yeast and the springy-sassy feel of newly risen bread when I punch it down. I'm all in favor of a hot, home-cooked meal on the table when I fall gratefully through the door at night.

Aye, there's the rub. When I fall through the door, three men and a ravenous dog are usually there, waiting for me to perform miracles with a package of rock-hard pork chops they forgot to take out of the freezer. On days like this, speed is what I seek. Next to a microwave oven, a can opener can be a cook's best friend. Times like these are why the Jolly Green Giant, Mr. Campbell (the soup man), Mrs. Wright (of cake mix fame) and the Pillsbury Dough Boy are all living high off the hog, as it were. It is their avowed purpose in life to bail out people like us, and I say, "let 'em."

True, I'd still do anything to avoid eating canned peas, and I think the people who invented frozen carrots have a thing or two to learn, but much can be done with a can of soup, a tin of tuna and a package of refrigerated dough.

Buy a good can opener. Sharpen your frozen food knife. Go for it.

WHAT EMERGENCY? One of the first cookbooks I ever read had a catchy section entitled "The Emergency Shelf" in which the smart cook was advised to forestall culinary disaster by investing in such gastronomic essentials as a jar of quail's eggs, a tin of herring in tomato sauce and a box of water crackers.

As few emergencies could be bad enough to make me eat that stuff, I invented my own ration pack of fast, good food. It had Cheez Whiz, which had been freshly invented in those days (a sobering thought in itself, considering how old that makes me); Ritz crackers; many pickles, especially olives; a batch of frozen brownies and a box of Nestle's Quik. No matter what disaster fate held in store, I knew I could cope, thus fortified.

Therein lies the secret of the classic emergency shelf: first, define the emergency. Is it for personal emergencies only–insomnia, a broken romance, a dented fender? Income tax? In that case it requires only your own fixers and comforters. A box of Callebaut chocolates? Maybe a bottle of good scotch? Maybe both, to be on the safe side?

My personal and current emergency shelf resides entirely in the refrigerator and consists of a tube of breadsticks, a hermetically-sealed tin of Camembert cheese, a half-bottle of good chardonnay and a pint of Häagen Dazs strawberry ice cream. Any emergency requiring more comfort than this is too terrible for me to think about.

The general emergency is more complex, as you may be called upon to feed assorted friends, relatives, their various children and pets. Any occasion with five or more people arriving concurrently or in tandem constitutes a general emergency. If you can't run away, you'll have to cook. Strategy is called for:

IN THE CUPBOARD: Always have a box of biscuit mix for making dumplings, and for faking domesticity with an afternoon tea or a farmhouse breakfast.

Keep a lot of canned soup around, including nacho cheese flavor which can get you through emergencies of a vaguely Mexican nature.

Keep dried onion soup on hand because almost any piece of meat will taste better sprinkled with this.

Canned beans are handy–garbanzos, kidney beans and traditional pork and beans. Also have ketchup, chili powder, three or four shapes of pasta and at least one jar of good spaghetti sauce.

Don't worry about tinned artichoke bottoms, jars of quail eggs, turtle meat and other exotica–they're expensive and about as useful as canned eye of newt.

Be sure to have garlic and onions; no kitchen can survive very long without them.

A bottle of maple syrup and an extra jar of peanut butter are sheer genius.

On pain of death, never run out of tuna.

IN THE REFRIGERATOR: Cheese (Cheddar and mozzarella) is essential. So are eggs, yogurt and real butter.

Keeping refrigerated dough for sudden bread, buns and cookies is an inspired move.

If you have apples and lemons (or oranges) plus fresh ginger, you can concoct terrific desserts in 30 minutes.

IN THE FREEZER: Puff pastry for impressive bits of culinary sleight-of-hand. Chicken breasts and pork tenderloin for fast stir-frys. Ground beef in small packages. Frozen mushrooms and baby peas. A small container of fabulous ice cream.

IN THE CELLAR: While a modest stock of spiritous beverages is not exactly essential, it can't hurt. One bottle each of decent red French burgundy, California chardonnay, French champagne and one dry sherry will look after most situations. Further investments are a good brandy and some scotch.

APPLIANCES I'D KILL FOR: The cook who is often faced with sudden meals should have a good food processor for soups, sauces, slicing, kneading and all other speed-of-light chores; a basic mircrowave for thawing and fast cooking; an ice cream maker for the world's best desserts with the least effort.

In this chapter we look at recipes for those times when you want to shout, "Help! Help!"

Saucy Yogurt Dip with Herbs

These days, I couldn't get along without yogurt, and this all-purpose sauce/dip is one of my favorite standbys. High in nutrition, low in calories, it can be used as a dressing for tuna or shrimp salad, as a dip for raw vegetables or baked potatoes. Use fresh herbs of your choice–I like to mix dill, parsley and basil for a tomato or green vegetable sauce, but a few sprigs of fresh tarragon are wonderful when it's chicken or fish. If you don't have access to fresh herbs, use smaller amounts of dry herbs to taste.

It keeps for a week in the refrigerator, and the recipe can be doubled.

2 cups	skim milk yogurt	500 mL
1/3 cup	Creamy Cucumber dressing, lo-cal	75 mL
1	clove garlic, mashed	1
1	green onion, minced	1
1/2 cup	fresh herbs, minced	125 mL
1/2 tsp	seasoned salt	2 mL

Stir all ingredients together at least 1 hour ahead of serving so flavors will have a chance to blend. Serve with vegetable crudites–carrots, green, red and yellow sweet peppers, cauliflower and sliced raw fennel. It also makes a lovely, light sauce for blanched snow peas, new baby peas, green beans or asparagus. Makes 3 cups.

Singapore Chicken Salad

When leftovers present themselves in sufficient quantities, make a salad. Use any crisp-leaved greens you have handy–romaine lettuce, Chinese cabbage, green or red cabbage. And pea pods are a nice touch if you have them.

DRESSING

2 tbsp	sugar	30 mL
3/4 cup	vegetable oil	175 mL
3 tbsp	sesame oil	45 mL
3 tbsp	vinegar	45 mL
2 tsp	soya sauce	10 mL
1 tsp	fresh ginger, grated	5 mL
	flavor packet from soup pkg	

SALAD

3 oz	pkg oriental soup noodles	85 g
4 cups	salad greens, shredded	1 L
1	carrot, shredded	1
2 or 3	green onions, sliced	2 or 3
2 cups	pea pods, blanched (optional)	500 mL
	leftover chicken, any amount, shredded	
1/4 cup	almonds, slivered	50 mL

Put dressing ingredients in a screw-top jar and shake to combine. Break dry (uncooked) soup noodles into chunks in a small bowl and pour dressing over. Let stand while preparing greens. (Do not let noodles get soggy–they should just soften slightly.)

Combine everything else except optional peapods in a bowl. Pour noodles and dressing over salad and toss well. To serve, mound salad on a small platter and garnish the edge with pea pods. Serves 6.

Note: Leftover peas may be added to this salad.

Spinach Squares

This spinach recipe came from a high school cafeteria manager who knew how to get kids to eat spinach. It goes over just as well with adults.

2	large eggs, beaten	2
10 oz	pkg frozen spinach	284 g
1	green onion, minced	1
4 tbsp	butter	60 mL
1 cup	Cheddar cheese, grated	250 mL
1 cup	milk	250 mL
3/4 cup	flour	175 mL
1 tsp	salt	5 mL
1 tsp	baking powder	5 mL

Preheat oven to 350 F (180 C). Grease a 9 x 13 inch (3 L) baking pan. Chop spinach and run under cold water to thaw. Squeeze to drain.

Combine all ingredients, mixing thoroughly. Spread mixture evenly in the pan and bake 45 minutes. Let sit 5 minutes before cutting into squares. Serve with a salad and crusty bread. Serves 6.

Oven Pot Roast

Nothing smells so welcoming on a hectic day as a slow-cooked pot roast.

5 lb	chuck roast	2.5 kg
1 1/2 oz	pkg dehydrated onion soup	45 g
10 oz	can mushroom soup	284 mL
3	carrots, chunked	3
1	small rutabaga, chunked	1
3	potatoes, halved	3

Preheat oven to 325 F (160 C). Place meat in a dutch oven or small roasting pan. Mix dry soup and undiluted mushroom soup together. (Mixture will be thick.) Spoon around roast, cover and cook 2 hours. Add vegetables and return to the oven for another hour. Serves 6.

Scalloped Hash Browns

When there's no time to cook from scratch, get out the frozen spuds and good old mushroom soup. This recipe was a winner in The *Edmonton Journal's* Convenience Recipe Contest.

4 cups	frozen hash browns	1 L
2	green onions, chopped	2
1/2 cup	whipped salad dressing	125 mL
10 oz	can mushroom soup	284 mL
3/4 cup	Cheddar cheese, grated	175 mL
1 tsp	salt	5 ml
1/2 tsp	pepper	2 ml
	milk to cover	

Preheat oven to 350 F (180 C). Butter a 2 qt (2 L) baking dish. Put hashbrowns in a colander and partially thaw by running under cold water.

Put hashbrowns, chopped onion, whipped salad dressing and grated cheese in the casserole. Stir in mushroom soup, salt and pepper, and add enough milk to come just to the top of potatoes.

Bake 40 to 50 minutes, or until bubbly. Stir once or twice during baking. (Do not let potatoes dry out.) Serves 4 to 6.

Note: For extra color and flavor, add 1 grated carrot or 1 small sweet pepper, red or green, finely diced.

Pork Chop Vegetable Dinner

The combination of fruit, vegetables and pork chops is unbeatable.

1 tbsp	vegetable oil	15 mL
8	boneless loin pork chops	8
2 cups	chicken broth	500 mL
1	sweet green pepper, sliced	1
1	medium carrot, thinly sliced	1
1	apple, peeled and sliced	1
1 tbsp	flour	15 mL

Heat oil in a large frypan. Brown pork chops on both sides. Remove, pour off oil, then return to the pan. Add broth and season lightly (bouillon cubes or granules tend to be salty). Cover, reduce heat to low and simmer 45 minutes.

Add green pepper, carrot and apple. Cover and simmer until carrots are tender.

Meanwhile place flour with 4 tbsp (60 mL) water in a small screw-cap jar. Shake vigorously to blend. Gradually stir into hot pan juices and cook until thick. Serve with steamed rice or noodles. Serves 4.

Biscuit Mix

This is a basic, inexpensive biscuit mix devised by Norma Bannerman and Donna Joy Halliday, authors of *Cooking with Cents*. Make it ahead of time and store for fast tea biscuits, shortcakes or other emergency baking sessions. This may be used instead of commercial mixes in any recipe calling for biscuit mix.

8 cups	flour	2 L
5 tbsp	baking powder	75 mL
1 tbsp	salt	15 mL
2 cups	shortening, chilled	500 mL

Combine flour, baking powder and salt in a large bowl. Blend well, folding while turning the bowl.

Cut shortening into large chunks and add to dry ingredients. Mix with a pastry blender until shortening is in fine particles. (Mixture should resemble coarse corn meal.) Label and store at room temperature in an air-tight container no longer than 2 months. Makes 3 batches/loaves.

Baking Powder Biscuits

| 3 cups | recipe Biscuit Mix | 750 mL |
| 3/4 | cup milk | 175 mL |

Preheat oven to 425 F (220 C). Add milk and stir with a fork. Dough should be soft, but not sticky. If extra flour is left in the bowl, add a very small amount of milk. Put dough on a board and knead lightly five or six times. Roll out to about 1/2 inch (1 cm) thickness. Cut into 12 squares.

Bake 12 to 15 minutes, or until golden brown. Makes 12 large biscuits.

Hurry Curry Crescent Pie

Here's a fast supper using handy refrigerated dough. 20 minutes should have it on the table.

1 lb	ground beef	500 g
1/2 cup	onion, chopped	125 mL
3/4 cup	sour cream	175 mL
2 tbsp	ketchup	30 mL
1 tsp	Dijon mustard	5 mL
1 tsp	curry powder	5 mL
1 tbsp	flour	15 mL
10 oz	can mushroom stems and pieces, drained	282 mL
1 cup	frozen peas	125 mL
8 oz	tube crescent dinner rolls	227 g
	dill pickles	
	tomato wedges	

Preheat oven to 375 F (190 C). Brown beef and onion. Drain thoroughly. Stir in remaining ingredients except crescent dough, dill pickles and tomato wedges. Let simmer 5 minutes. Do not boil.

Meanwhile, separate crescent dough into 8 triangles. Arrange triangles, spoke-fashion, in an ungreased 9 inch (22 cm) pie plate, with narrow tips of triangles extended over edge.

Spoon meat mixture into dough-lined plate. Bring tips of dough triangles over filling to center.

Bake about 12 minutes, or until golden brown. Cut into wedges and garnish each serving with additional sour cream, a slice of pickle and tomato wedge. Serves 6.

Cheddar-Corn Scones

For these scrumptious hot scones I use the Biscuit Mix in this chapter. If you haven't any on hand, use a commercial mix.

2 1/2 cups	recipe Biscuit Mix	625 mL
1/2 tsp	salt	2 mL
1/2 tsp	dry mustard	2 mL
1 cup	Cheddar cheese, grated	250 mL
10 oz	can creamed corn	284 ml
1	egg, beaten	1
1 tbsp	milk	15 mL

Preheat oven to 425 F (220 C). In a medium bowl, combine biscuit mix, salt and dry mustard. With a fork, stir in cheese, creamed corn and egg until a soft dough forms. (Dough should be soft but manageable. If stiff, add some milk.) Turn onto a floured surface. Knead gently 10 to 12 times until no longer sticky. Roll or press dough to a 1 inch (2 cm) thickness.

    Cut into 10 wedge-shaped scones. Place scones 1 inch (2 cm) apart on an ungreased cookie sheet. Brush with milk. Bake 12 to 15 minutes, or until golden brown. Serve warm. Makes 10 large scones.

Easy Cheese Dill Bread

Serve this bread warm with your favorite soup. Use your own biscuit mix or a commercial mix. If you have fresh dillweed in the garden, add up to 1/4 cup (50 mL), chopped, in place of the dry.

1/2 cup	Cheddar cheese, grated	125 mL
2 1/2 cups	recipe Biscuit Mix	625 mL
1 cup	milk	250 mL
1 tbsp	dry dillweed	15 mL

Preheat oven to 400 F (200 C). Grease a 4 cup (1 L) ring mold or a 9 inch (2 L) loaf pan. Stir cheese into other ingredients. (Do not overmix.) Spoon into the baking pan. Bake about 45 minutes, or until golden. Cool 10 minutes in the pan before removing. Serve warm with butter. Serves 8.

Sweetened Condensed Milk

This has been one of my most requested microwave recipes. Use it in any recipe calling for sweetened condensed milk.

1/2 cup	honey	125 mL
1/4 cup	water	50 mL
1/4 cup	butter	50 mL
1 cup	dry nonfat milk	250 mL

In a 2 cup (500 mL) measuring cup, combine honey, water and butter. Microwave 2 minutes on high power, or until mixture boils, stirring every 30 seconds. Pour hot mixture into a blender and add dry milk crystals. Process until smooth. Refrigerate until needed. Recipe may be doubled. Makes 1 cup (250 mL).

Note: To make this without a microwave oven, bring honey, water and butter to boil in a saucepan. Then blend as directed.

Angel Food Dessert

Here's a dessert to make ahead of time that's both easy and delicious. Another winner from an *Edmonton Journal* Convenience Recipe Contest.

1	angel food cake	1
5	Crispy Crunch bars	5
2 cups	whipping cream	500 mL
1 tsp	vanilla	5 mL

Slice cake into 2 layers. Break 4 chocolate bars into very small pieces. Do not crush. Whip cream until stiff and fold in chocolate bar bits.

Place bottom layer on serving plate. Spread with about 1/3 cream mixture. Place remaining layer on top, then ice top and sides of cake, using all remaining cream mixture. Crumble last chocolate bar and sprinkle on top of cake. Refrigerate about 5 hours to let flavors blend. Serves 8.

FAST TRACK MENU

Quick Cheese Sticks
New Orleans Bouillabaisse
Mascarpone with Rummy Raisins

You're home at six, the kids are hungry, there's a meeting at seven and you still have to pick up the dog from the vet. Here's a meal to solve the problem immediately.

Quick Cheese Sticks

4	hot dog buns	4
1/2 cup	butter	125 mL
1/2 cup	Parmesan cheese, finely grated	125 mL
1/2 cup	Cheddar cheese, finely grated	125 mL

Preheat oven to 375 F (190 C). Slice each bun into 4 lengthwise strips. Put butter into a 9 x 13 inch (3 L) cake pan and let melt in the oven. Mix cheeses together on a plate.

When butter has melted, roll cut sides of buns in butter, then dip in cheese. Return to pan, cheese-side up. Bake 10 minutes. Serves 4.

New Orleans Bouillabaisse

On a cool evening, this makes a fast, warming supper.

1/2 lb	frozen snapper filets	250 g
1/2 lb	frozen shrimp	250 g
6 1/2 oz	can chunk tuna	184 g
2 cups	canned tomatoes	500 mL
1 cup	water	250 mL
1 cup	frozen mixed vegetables	250 mL
1/2 tsp	each, salt, thyme and garlic powder	2 mL
dash	Tabasco sauce	dash

Partially thaw snapper in cold water. Cut into cubes. Combine tomatoes, frozen vegetables and seasonings in a large pot. Bring to simmer. Add snapper and simmer 15 minutes. Add shrimp and tuna and simmer 10 minutes more. Ladle into big bowls and serve with cheese sticks. Serves 4 generously.

Mascarpone with Rummy Raisins

Put this simple dessert together before dinner and it will be ready to eat with your coffee. (Mascarpone is available at good Italian delis.)

1/2 cup	seedless raisins	125 mL
1/3 cup	rum	75 mL
2 cups	mascarpone cheese	500 mL
2 tbsp	honey	30 mL
1 tsp	instant coffee granules	5 mL
	plain cookies	
	fresh fruit in season	

Place raisins and rum in a cup and let soak.

Briskly beat mascarpone with honey and coffee. Pour rummy raisins into mixture and stir. Refrigerate during dinner. To serve, scoop about 1/2 cup (125 mL) cheese mixture onto a small plate. Add a couple of plain cookies and a wedge or two of fruit (bananas, winter pears or apples are delicious with this combination). Spread cookies with mascarpone and eat with fruit. This is lovely with real espresso. Serves 4, with leftovers.

Note: You may substitute 1/3 cup (75 mL) fruit juice for the rum.

CHAPTER 4
April

Let Them Eat Cake

April Recipes

Marie Antoinette was having a bad day. Put yourself in her place.

It's an impromptu press conference, a typical scrum, with pushy reporters crowding around the royal coach, yelling rude questions, scaring the horses, everybody talking at once. Then, from the crowd:

"Hey, Marie, what's the story on the peasants? They say they have no bread. What are you and Louis prepared to do about it?"

And she answered (so rumor has it), "Let them eat cake."

Now it may be that Marie was having her own problems. Maybe the footmen had slept in, or her wig hadn't come back from the cleaners. Who knows? After all, she could have said worse.

She could have said, "Those (bleep bleep) PEASANTS again! They're NEVER happy! Whaddaya EXPECT me to do about it? WHAT?"

And who would have remembered that little outburst?

Oh, there'd have been the usual whining among the town criers about her cavalier attitude and her unfeeling contempt for those less fortunate. But the next day Louis would have said something equally gauche, and all would have been forgiven and forgotten.

In fact, she'd likely have gotten away with it if she'd told them to eat boiled cabbage, or liver or some other dish nobody really loved in the first place. She could have said, "Let them eat tripe!"

But she had to mention cake.

With a single sentence she turned cake into a social issue. Cake–the dish that is, was, and ever shall be the universal party food. We can't have a birthday without it. Can't get married, or christened, or celebrate Twelfth Night, or cheer on the Grey Cup. Everybody loves cake, and when somebody else gets more than we do, we get miserable.

Proof: Wave a fat slice of double chocolate cheesecake under the nose of a dieting friend and see what happens to your friendship.

In this chapter, you can eat all the cake you want and a slice of pie for chasers. Enjoy.

Chocolate Beet Cake

When I first sampled this at a market I could hardly believe what was in it–beets!

2 cups	all-purpose flour, unsifted	500 mL
2 cups	sugar	500 mL
1 cup	water	250 mL
3/4 cup	plain yogurt	175 mL
1/4 cup	soft butter	50 mL
1 1/4 tsp	baking soda	6 mL
1 tsp	salt	5 mL
1 tsp	vanilla	5 mL
1/2 tsp	baking powder	2 mL
2	eggs	2
4 oz	unsweetened baking chocolate, melted	125 g
1 1/2 cups	cooked beets, grated	375 g

Preheat oven to 350 F (180 C). Measure all ingredients into a large bowl and beat 1 minute at low speed, scraping sides of the bowl constantly. Then beat 3 minutes at highest speed. Pour into a greased and floured 9 x 13 inch (3 L) pan.
  Bake 45 to 50 minutes. Serve warm with whipped cream. Serves 8.

Honey Pecan Pie

Honey and pecans together–what could be better?

1 cup	honey	250 mL
3	eggs, beaten	3
2 tbsp	sugar	30 mL
1/4 cup	powdered skim milk	50 mL
1/4 cup	butter	50 mL
1 1/2 cups	pecans	375 mL
1/2 tsp	vanilla	2 mL
9 inch	unbaked pastry shell	22 cm

Preheat oven to 350 F (180 C). Mix honey with well-beaten eggs. Cream sugar, powdered skim milk and butter, and add to honey-egg mixture. Stir in pecans and vanilla. Pour into unbaked pie shell and bake about 1 hour, or until the toothpick test shows center to be done. Serves 6.

Carrot Cake with Cream Cheese Frosting

Who better to trust for a great carrot cake recipe than the carrot grower who supplied this one?

CAKE

2 cups	all-purpose flour, unsifted	500 mL
2 cups	sugar	500 mL
2 tsp	baking soda	10 mL
1 tsp	salt	5 mL
1 tbsp	cinnamon	15 mL
4	eggs	4
1 cup	corn oil	250 mL
1 cup	golden raisins	250 mL
4 cups	raw carrots, finely grated	1 L

Preheat oven to 350 F (180 C). Butter and flour a 9 x 13 inch (3 L) cake pan.

Mix together flour, sugar, soda, salt and cinnamon. Set aside. In a large mixing bowl, beat eggs until frothy. Slowly beat in oil. Gradually add flour mixture, beating until smooth. Add raisins and carrots, and stir well.

Pour into prepared cake pan. Bake 55 to 60 minutes, or until it passes the toothpick test. Cool in pan.

FROSTING

8 oz	cream cheese, softened	250 g
4 tbsp	butter	60 mL
2 cups	icing sugar	500 mL
2 tsp	lemon juice	10 mL
1 tsp	vanilla	5 mL
1/2 cup	pecans, chopped	125 mL

Combine all ingredients except pecans. Beat until smooth. Frost cake and sprinkle with chopped pecans. Serves 12.

Bacardi Cake

I've adored this rummy cake ever since a neighbor who worked for the Bacardi company shared a slightly different version of the recipe with me one Christmas.

CAKE

18 oz	pkg golden cake mix	520 g
3 oz	pkg instant vanilla pudding	92 g
4	large eggs	4
1/2 cup	vegetable oil	125 mL
2/3 cup	rum	150 mL
1/3 cup	water	75 mL

Preheat oven to 350 F (180 C). Butter and flour a bundt pan or 9 inch (2 L) tube pan.

With the mixer on low speed, beat all ingredients about 2 minutes. Pour into prepared pan. Bake 45 to 50 minutes or until an inserted toothpick comes out clean. Let cake rest in the pan 10 minutes before inverting onto a wire rack. Glaze cake while still warm.

GLAZE

1/4 cup	rum	50 mL
1 tbsp	lemon juice	15 mL
1 tsp	lemon peel, grated	5 mL
1/4 cup	water	50 mL
1 cup	white sugar	250 mL
1/3 cup	butter	75 mL

In a small saucepan, mix together rum, lemon juice, lemon peel, water, sugar and butter. Boil until sugar has dissolved. While cake is still warm, poke random holes in top with a toothpick and drizzle glaze over top and down sides. Serves 10.

Double Chocolate Cheesecake

If you're a chocoholic, this one's for you.

CRUST

1 1/2 cups	chocolate wafer crumbs	375 mL
1/4 cup	unsalted butter, melted	50 mL

Preheat oven to 350 F (180 C). Combine all ingredients and press firmly into a 9 inch (2 L) springform pan. Bake 5 minutes. Cool.

CHEESECAKE FILLING

1 lb	cream cheese	500 g
1/3 cup	sugar	75 mL
2	eggs	2
1/2 cup	sour cream	125 mL
2 tbsp	unsalted butter, melted	30 mL
1/2 tsp	vanilla	2 mL
1/2 cup	semisweet chocolate chips, melted	125 mL

Preheat oven to 350 F (180 C). Beat together cheese, sugar and eggs. Blend in sour cream, melted butter and vanilla, and pour onto crust. Spoon on melted chocolate and spiral into batter with a knife. Bake 30 to 45 minutes, or until set. Chill.

MOUSSE FILLING

2 cups	semisweet chocolate chips	500 mL
1/3 cup	boiling water	75 mL
5	egg yolks	5
3 tbsp	brandy	45 mL
4 tbsp	unsalted butter, melted	60 mL
5	egg whites	5

In a food processor or blender, process chocolate chips 5 seconds. Add boiling water slowly and continue to process. Add egg yolks 1 at a time. Add brandy and butter a little at a time.

Beat egg whites until stiff and gently fold into chocolate. Pour onto cheesecake and refrigerate 4 to 6 hours.

TOPPING

Melt 2 squares semisweet chocolate and drizzle over top of cake. Sprinkle with chopped nuts (almonds, walnuts or pecans). Chill. Serves 12 to 14.

White Chocolate Coconut Cheesecake

White chocolate, coconut and almonds are a heavenly combination in this cloud of a dessert.

CRUST

3/4 cup	sliced almond	175 mL
6	bakery coconut macaroons	6
6 tbsp	butter, melted	90 mL
2 tbsp	sugar	30 mL
1/2 tsp	cinnamon	2 mL

Toast almonds by baking in a single layer on a nonstick baking sheet at 400 F (200 C) about 4 minutes, watching closely. Crumble macaroons. (If they seem small, use 8 instead of 6.)

Preheat oven to 350 F (180 C). Combine macaroon crumbs with melted butter, then toss with almonds. Pat into bottom of a greased 9 inch (2 L) springform pan. Bake at 10 minutes, or until starting to turn golden. Remove from oven and cool slightly. Mix sugar and cinnamon, and sprinkle on crust just before pouring in cheese filling.

FILLING

1 tbsp	unflavored gelatin	15 mL
1/4 cup	milk	50 mL
1 cup	cream cheese	250 mL
3/4 cup	icing sugar, sifted	175 mL
6 oz	white chocolate, melted	210 g
1 1/2 cups	whipping cream	375 mL
1 tsp	coconut flavoring	5 mL
2 tbsp	light rum	30 mL

In a small pan, sprinkle gelatin over milk and heat, stirring until gelatin is dissolved. Beat cream cheese until smooth. Beat in sugar and melted white chocolate. Gradually beat in gelatin mixture. Refrigerate briefly while preparing cake.

Whip cream until soft peaks form. Beat in coconut flavoring and rum. Fold whipped cream mixture into cream cheese and chocolate mixture. Pour into cooled crust. Refrigerate 5 to 6 hours before removing from pan. Garnish with toasted coconut or white chocolate curls. Serves 12 to 14.

Sour Cream Apple Pie

A Dutch cook just arrived from Amsterdam shared this with me.

9 inch	pie shell, unbaked	22 cm
2/3 cup	brown sugar	150 mL
1 tsp	cinnamon	5 mL
1/4 tsp	nutmeg, freshly grated	1 mL
1/4 tsp	salt	1 mL
2 tbsp	cornstarch	30 mL
8	apples, peeled, cored and sliced	8
1 cup	sour cream	250 mL
1/2 cup	flour	125 mL
3 tbsp	white sugar	45 mL
3 tbsp	brown sugar	45 mL
1 tsp	cinnamon	5 mL
1/4 cup	butter, melted	50 mL

Preheat oven to 425 F (220 C). Combine brown sugar, cinnamon, nutmeg, salt and cornstarch. Sprinkle alternately over apples layered in crust. Cover with sour cream.

For topping, mix together flour, white sugar, brown sugar, cinnamon and melted butter. (Mixture will be crumbly.) Sprinkle over pie. Bake 10 minutes. Reduce heat to 375 F (190 C) and bake 35 to 40 minutes. Serve warm with vanilla ice cream. Serves 6.

Cranberry Raisin Pie with Yogurt Topping

This pie tastes like cherries, and the cranberries have a lovely poppy texture.

PIE

4 cups	frozen cranberries	1 L
14 oz	can raisin pie filling	398 mL
1/2 tsp	almond extract	2 mL
1/2 cup	sugar	125 mL
9 inch	2 pie crusts	1 L

Preheat oven to 375 F (190 C). Let cranberries defrost 15 minutes at room temperature. In a large bowl, fold together cranberries, raisin pie filling, almond extract and sugar. Pour into prepared pie crusts and top with yogurt topping. Bake 45 to 50 minutes, or until cranberries bubble through topping here and there. Cool completely before serving.

TOPPING

2 cups	plain yogurt	500 mL
1	egg	1
1 tsp	almond extract	5 mL
1 tbsp	sugar	15 mL
2 tbsp	flour	30 mL

Mix together and spoon over unbaked pies, dividing equally. Makes 2 pies.

Mud Pie

Mud pie came from an enterprising chef whose name may be forgotten, but whose fans are legion. Everybody loves it.

24	Oreo cookies	24
1/3 cup	butter, melted	75 mL
4 cups	coffee ice cream	1 L
3 tsp	instant coffee granules	15 mL
4 tsp	water	20 mL
2 tbsp	liquid honey	30 mL
4 tsp	butter, cut in pieces	20 mL
3/4 cup	semisweet chocolate chips	175 mL
1/2 cup	whipping cream	125 mL
2 tbsp	coffee liqueur	30 mL
	shaved chocolate curls for garnish	

In a food processor or blender, process cookies and melted butter into coarse crumbs. Press firmly into a 9 inch (22 cm) pie plate. Freeze until firm.

Slightly soften ice cream. Spoon into crust. Return to freezer 1 hour.

Bring coffee, water, honey and butter to simmer. Remove from heat and add chocolate chips, stirring until melted. Let cool.

Drizzle chocolate glaze over ice cream, swirling with the back of a spoon to create a marbled pattern. Return to freezer until ready to serve.

Before serving, whip cream. When nearly stiff, beat in coffee liqueur. Mound generously over pie. Sprinkle with shaved chocolate. Serves 8.

Frozen Peanut Crunch Cake

The grand prize winner in one *Edmonton Journal* Favorite Recipe Contest was Lynne Hurley, whose cake is one of the best peanut butter desserts I've ever tasted.

CRUST

1/4 cup	peanut butter	50 mL
1/4 cup	butter, melted	50 mL
1 1/2 cups	chocolate wafer crumbs	375 mL
1/2 cup	unsalted peanuts, finely chopped	125 mL

Preheat oven to 375 F (190 C). Melt butter and peanut butter over low heat. Mix all ingredients together in a small bowl. Press into bottom of a greased 9 inch (2 L) springform pan. Bake crust 10 minutes. Let cool completely, then chill 15 minutes before filling.

FILLING

8 cups	vanilla ice cream	2 L
1 cup	peanut brittle, crushed	250 mL
3/4 cup	peanut butter	175 mL

Soften ice cream for about 1/2 an hour. Scoop 1/3 ice cream into prepared crust. Swirl 1/3 peanut butter into ice cream and then sprinkle with 1/3 brittle. Repeat layers until pie is full.

Freeze at least 4 hours, covered. Remove from freezer 10 to 15 minutes before serving for easier cutting. Top with warm sauce.

SAUCE

1/4 cup	semisweet chocolate	50 mL
1/2 cup	milk	125 mL
1/2 cup	brown sugar	125 mL
1/2 tsp	vanilla	2 mL
1/3 cup	peanut butter	75 mL

Melt chocolate in a double boiler. Add milk and brown sugar, heating and stirring until sugar is dissolved. Add peanut butter and continue heating until sauce is thick and smooth. Stir in vanilla and remove from heat. Serve warm. Serves 8 to 10.

FAST TRACK MENU

Stuffed Potatoes
Turtle Cake

Stuffed Potatoes

Stuffed spuds made in your microwave are a terrific one-dish meal. Prepare them while your Turtle Cake is baking.

8	baking potatoes	8
10 oz	can creamed corn	284 mL
6 1/2 oz	can tuna	184 g
1	green onion, chopped	1
pinch	each, salt and pepper	pinch
1 1/4 cup	Cheddar cheese, grated	300 mL

Bake potatoes in the microwave. Cool slightly. Slit potatoes crosswise. Carefully spoon out potato, leaving enough inside to support skin.

In a medium bowl, combine potato, corn, drained tuna, green onion, salt and pepper. Spoon mixture into potato skins. Place in a shallow greased baking dish. Microwave 10 minutes on high power. Sprinkle with cheese. Return to microwave until cheese is melted and bubbly. Serves 8.

Turtle Cake

So easy, so scrumptious, and one of the reasons I'm forever falling off my perpetual diet.

18 oz	pkg German chocolate cake mix	520 g
1/2 cup	butter, softened	125 mL
1 1/2 cups	water	375 mL
1/2 cup	vegetable oil	125 mL
1 1/4 cup	sweetened condensed milk	300 mL
1 cup	pecans, chopped	250 mL
1 lb	caramels	500 g

Preheat oven to 350 F (180 C). Combine chocolate cake mix, butter, water, oil and 1/2 sweetened condensed milk in mixing bowl. With a wire whisk, beat until blended. Pour 1/2 batter into a greased and floured 9 x 13 inch (3 L) cake pan. Reserve remaining batter. Bake 20 to 25 minutes.

   Melt caramels and mix together with remaining condensed milk over low heat until smooth. Immediately spread over baked cake while still warm. Sprinkle generously with pecans. Cover with reserved cake batter. Return to oven and bake 25 to 35 minutes longer, or until cake tests done. Cool. Spread with chocolate frosting, or dust icing sugar over top. Serves 8 generously.

CHAPTER 5
May

The Rites of Spring

May Recipes

For many people, the first rite of spring is picking a dandelion. For me, it's the return of the ice cream man wending his way through suburban streets with his music-box version of Lara's Theme playing full blast, one note slightly off key.

Never mind that there's still snow melting in the lane, and we could have one more blizzard, maybe two. The ice cream man cometh, *ergo*, spring has sprung.

But there's more to ice cream than simply eating it. There's art involved. You have to know what you're about.

HOW TO INDULGE

The fine art of indulging in ice cream is best observed in little kids who instinctively demand banana splits even though no child has ever been known to finish one.

To do it right, you must first find a proper diner, one of the old-time joints where they serve real milkshakes instead of frozen cake batter. Note: If you can't smell onions frying, this is not a real diner. LEAVE AT ONCE.

But, given that the place smells good and has the requisite number of counter stools, park yourself where you can supervise the assembly of a classic banana split.

Here's how: Three scoops of ice cream—chocolate first, vanilla nestled in the middle, then strawberry. That's for starters.

Next, a large dollop of pineapple sauce (NOT runny, crushed pineapple, which indicates cheapskate management); a big scoop of strawberry sauce; a good smash of chocolate sauce. An entire banana, peeled and split while you watch, should now be propped on either side of the ice cream like a couple of logs.

The whole thing will be smothered in cream that has been whipped into submission in one of those metal shakers and followed by a generous blizzard of chocolate sprinkles. Finally, a maraschino cherry WITH stem, or possibly two. Yum. Dig in.

If you're still on your feet when the platter is clean, you might consider a strawberry sundae. Or a hot fudge. Classics, one and all.

Fresh Fruit Gazpacho

3	large, ripe tomatoes	3
3 cups	freshly squeezed orange juice	750 mL
1 tbsp	sugar	15 mL
2 tsp	orange peel, grated	10 mL
1	each, cantaloupe, honeydew and papaya, peeled, seeded and cubed	1
1	large apple, unpeeled, cored and cubed	1
1 cup	fresh strawberries, halved	250 mL
1 cup	fresh blueberries	250 ml
1	kiwi, peeled and sliced	1
	fresh mint for garnish	

Peel tomatoes and cut in chunks. In a food processor or blender purée tomatoes. Add orange juice, sugar, grated orange peel, 1/2 cantaloupe, honeydew and papaya cubes. Process until smooth.

Pour into a large serving bowl. Stir in remaining fruit. Cover. Chill 4 to 6 hours, or until very cold. If desired, garnish with fresh mint. Serves about 8 as a first course.

Strawberry Soup with Honey and Citrus

You can make strawberry soup with white wine, vodka or even champagne, but my favorite is this gentle version made with honey and buttermilk–perfect for brunch.

4 cups	fresh strawberries	1 L
1 cup	orange juice	250 mL
2 tsp	instant tapioca	10 mL
pinch	allspice	pinch
pinch	cinnamon	pinch
1/2 cup	honey	125 mL
1 tsp	lemon peel, grated	5 mL
1 tbsp	lemon juice	15 mL
1 cup	buttermilk	250 mL

Put strawberries in a blender and purée. Combine purée with orange juice in a saucepan. Remove about 1 1/4 cup (300 mL) of mixture and stir into tapioca. Add tapioca mixture to purée in the saucepan. Add allspice, cinnamon and honey. Cook, stirring until mixture thickens. Remove from heat, add lemon peel, lemon juice and buttermilk. Cover and refrigerate overnight. Serves 4.

Spring Harvest Chicken Soup

With this recipe, Donna Maurice won grand prize in an *Edmonton Journal* Recipe Contest. It's just as good the day after.

3 lb	broiler chicken	1.5 kg
2 cups	chicken broth	500 mL
8 cups	water	2 L
1	large onion, cut into chunks	1
1	clove garlic, halved	1
1/2 lb	asparagus	250 g
2	medium size leeks	2
1/4 lb	green beans	125 g
1/2 lb	peas in pod, shelled	250 g
1/4 lb	mushrooms, sliced	125 g
	salt and pepper to taste	
	toast rounds and herb mayonnaise	

Wash chicken. In a Dutch oven, combine chicken, broth, water, onion and garlic. Cover and simmer until thigh meat pulls easily from bone, about 45 minutes. Lift out chicken. When cool, pull meat into bite-size pieces. Set aside.

Return bones and skin to kettle, cover and simmer another 30 minutes. Pour soup through a strainer, discarding bones, skin and residue. Return soup to kettle.

Meanwhile snap off and discard tough asparagus ends, cut off tips and set aside. Cut stalks into 1 inch (2 cm) pieces. Trim off root ends of leeks and tough tops. Split leeks lengthwise, rinse well and thinly slice. Snap off and discard ends of beans and cut into 1 inch (2 cm) pieces.

Bring soup back to simmering. Add vegetables and simmer, uncovered, until bright green, 5 to 7 minutes. Add cooked chicken and heat through. Season with salt and pepper.

Spread toast rounds with herb mayonnaise and place in soup plates. Ladle in hot soup. Makes 4 qt (4 L) or 8 servings.

TOAST ROUNDS
Preheat oven to 350 F (180 C). Thinly slice 1 slender 8 oz (250 g) baguette and set in a single layer on baking sheets. Bake until toasted, about 15 minutes. Cool.

HERB MAYONNAISE
Combine 1 cup (250 mL) homemade or purchased mayonnaise, 1 clove garlic (minced or pressed), and 2 tsp (10 mL) chopped fresh herbs, such as rosemary, oregano, basil, thyme and marjoram. Cover and chill.

Spinach Salad with Steak and Strawberries

Just in time for strawberry season comes this colorful salad with its unusual combination.

1 lb	top or eye of round steak	500 g
2 tbsp	white wine vinegar	30 mL
1 tbsp	Worcestershire sauce	15 mL
1 tbsp	onion, finely chopped	15 mL
1 tbsp	sesame seeds	15 mL
1 tsp	sugar	5 mL
1	clove garlic	1
1/2 tsp	chili powder	2 mL
1/4 tsp	white pepper	1 mL
1 tbsp	vegetable oil	15 mL
1	bunch fresh spinach leaves, cleaned and stemmed	1
2	medium oranges, peeled and sectioned	2
2 cups	fresh strawberries, sliced	500 mL

Barbecue steak over medium hot coals, 5 to 6 minutes per side for rare, or until done to taste. Cut across grain into thin slices and place in a glass dish.

To prepare marinade, combine vinegar, Worcestershire sauce, onion, sesame seeds, sugar, garlic, chili powder and pepper.

Beat well with a wire whisk or in a blender. Gradually add oil, blending until smooth. Pour over steaks, cover and refrigerate 3 hours or more. Place spinach on a serving plate.

Arrange beef slices, oranges and strawberries on spinach. Drizzle with remaining marinade. Serves 4.

Antipasto Salad

Although iceberg lettuce has had some bad press, it's excellent in this salad because it's firm and crisp and can be cut into chunks. Antipasto salad will go well with your first barbecue of the season.

DRESSING

1 cup	olive oil	250 mL
2 tbsp	tarragon vinegar	30 mL
1 tbsp	fresh lemon juice	15 mL
	salt and pepper to taste	
1	clove garlic, finely minced	1
1 tsp	oregano	5 mL

Mix together oil, vinegar, lemon juice, salt, pepper, garlic and oregano.

SALAD

1	zucchini, thinly sliced	1
1/2	head cauliflower, broken into flowerets	1/2
2	green onions, chopped	2
1	head iceberg lettuce, chunked	1
4	large mushrooms, sliced	4
2	tomatoes, diced	2
12	pitted black olives	12
8 oz	Italian salami, sliced and cut into strips	250 g
4 oz	Provolone cheese, cut into strips	125 g
1 cup	seasoned croutons	250 mL
1/4 cup	Parmesan cheese, grated	50 mL

Put zucchini, cauliflower and green onions in a bowl and pour dressing over top. Toss lightly and refrigerate 8 hours or more.

Combine remaining ingredients, except croutons and Parmesan, in a large bowl and toss well. Add croutons and sprinkle cheese over top. Serves 8.

Melon Salad with Curry

Serve this easy, refreshing salad with grilled chicken or any spicy meat dish.

4 cups	melon balls, mixed	1 L
1 tsp	curry powder	5 mL
1 tbsp	fresh lemon juice	15 mL
1 tsp	honey	5 mL
1/2 cup	yogurt	125 mL
	watercress or cucumbers	

Mix curry powder, lemon juice and honey in a small bowl. Let dressing stand 5 minutes. Whip in yogurt. Stir curry mixture into yogurt, then fold in melon balls. Chill 10 minutes. Serve on a large plate or individual dishes. Garnish with watercress or cucumber slices. Winter pear may also be used. Serves 3 to 4.

Rhubarb Mint Sauce

Mint sauce is so traditional with lamb that other possibilities are usually ignored. Here's an excellent variation that's as good with chicken as it is with lamb.

4 cups	rhubarb, diced	1 L
4 cups	mint, chopped	1 L
4 cups	sugar	1 L
1/2 cup	red wine vinegar	125 mL

Place ingredients in a large pan and simmer about 1 hour, or until slightly thinner than jam. Pour into small sterilized jars and seal. Makes about 4 cups (4 L).

Chive Blossom Vinaigrette

One of the first flowers of spring is the pretty purple ball of the chive blossom. If you want extra color in this dressing, the shredded petals of a dandelion blossom may be added as well.

3	chive blossoms	3
1	egg yolk	1
1/3 cup	red wine vinegar	75 mL
1 tsp	sugar	5 mL
2	cloves garlic	2
	salt and ground pepper to taste	

Combine and mix all ingredients except blossoms in a mixer. When mixed, tear chive blossoms into dressing. Drizzle over cold roast duck or beef, or serve over mixed green salad with spring blossoms. Makes about 1/2 cup.

Pasta with Garlic, Basil and Tomato

I make this dish as soon as the first basil is in my garden. It's ridiculously simple and totally delicious. If you like red wine, drink a simple chianti or a chianti classico.

3	cloves garlic, crushed	3
1/4	cup extra virgin olive oil	50 mL
1 lb	spaghetti, cooked *al dente*	500 g
1	fresh tomato, peeled and chopped	1
1	handful of fresh basil leaves, minced	1
	pepper to taste, freshly ground	
1/2 cup	Parmesan cheese, freshly grated	125 mL

While pasta is cooking, fry garlic in oil until golden, taking care not to burn garlic.

Toss basil and tomatoes into hot oil and immediately pour sauce over drained, hot pasta. Sprinkle with pepper, toss with basil leaves, add Parmesan and toss again. Serve immediately. Serves 4 to 6.

Spring Vegetable Platter

8	small potatoes, scrubbed and halved	8
16	small carrots	16
1	bunch red radishes	1
2	bunches asparagus or green beans	2
	lemon wedges for garnish	
	fresh parsley, chopped, for garnish	

Boil unpeeled potatoes ahead of time in lightly salted water. When barely tender, drain, rinse quickly with cold water and reserve at room temperature, covered.

Scrub carrots and cook the same way, reserving in the same dish as potatoes.

About 15 minutes before serving, put potatoes and carrots in a pot big enough to hold them comfortably. Add 2 tbsp (30 mL) butter and 1/4 cup (50 mL) water. Cook over medium heat 5 minutes. Add trimmed, cleaned radishes. Cook 5 minutes more. (Radishes should be rosy pink and still crisp.)

Meanwhile place cleaned, trimmed asparagus or green beans in a steamer and bring water to rolling boil. Steam until bright green and just tender, about 5 minutes for slim stalks. Place in middle of a serving platter and rub with soft butter. Arrange other vegetables around asparagus. Drizzle with melted butter. Sprinkle with parsley and garnish with lemon wedges.

Note: Improvise a steamer by placing asparagus stalk in a tall coffee pot. Add 1 inch (2 cm) water and boil briskly. Serves 4 to 6.

Lamb Chops with Shallot Toast

The balsamic vinegar gives this sauce a slightly sweet flavor that's perfect with barbecued lamb. Serve with beaujolais.

SAUCE

3 tbsp	butter	45 mL
1 1/2 cup	shallots, chopped	375 mL
1/2 cup	balsamic vinegar	125 mL
1/2 cup	dry white wine	125 mL
2 tbsp	sugar	30 mL
1 1/2 tsp	parsley, minced	7 mL
1/2 tsp	black pepper, freshly ground	2 mL

Melt 3 tbsp (45 mL) butter in a heavy non-aluminum saucepan over medium-low heat. Add peeled, chopped shallots and cook until limp, about 8 minutes. Add vinegar, wine and sugar. Cook, stirring constantly, over high heat until reduced by half and slightly thickened, about 3 to 4 minutes. Add parsley and pepper, and stir to mix. Remove from heat. Strain sauce through fine sieve set over a bowl. Reserve liquid and solids separately.

TOAST

1 1/2 tsp	olive oil	7 mL
4 tbsp	butter, softened	60 mL
1/4 tsp	salt	1 mL
1	long loaf French bread	1

Put reserved shallot solids into a food processor with oil, 4 tbsp (60 mL) butter and salt. Blend until smooth.

Cut bread into 1/2 inch (1 cm) slices. Broil until golden on both sides. Spread 1 side with shallot mixture. Broil 6 inches (14 cm) from heat source, until browned, about 2 minutes.

LAMB

12	loin lamb chops, about 1 inch (2 cm) thick	12
	watercress for garnish	

Broil lamb chops about 6 inches (14 cm) from heat source, until medium rare, about 8 minutes, turning after 4 to 6 minutes. Reheat reserved shallot liquid. Pour over lamb chops on serving plate. Garnish with watercress and shallot toast. Serves 6.

Sautéed Seafood with Rhubarb-Ginger Sauce

This is one of those unusual dishes that result when good cooks play with unconventional combinations. Save it for a special occasion.

2	stalks red rhubarb, diced	2
2 tbsp	brown sugar	30 mL
1 tbsp	fresh orange juice	15 mL
1/4 tsp	orange peel, grated	1 mL
2 tsp	fresh ginger root, minced	10 mL
2 tbsp	granulated sugar	30 mL
2 tbsp	water	30 mL
1/2 cup	butter	125 mL
1/2 lb	scallops, rinsed	250 g
1/2 lb	shrimps, shelled	250 g
1/2 cup	dry vermouth	125 mL
1/2 cup	heavy cream	125 mL

Combine rhubarb, brown sugar, orange juice and peel, and cook until soft, about 20 minutes.

In a skillet, combine ginger root, granulated sugar and 2 tbsp (30 mL) water. Cook until reduced by half. Add butter.

Increase heat and add scallops and shrimp. Cook, stirring, until opaque, about 1 minute or less. Remove seafood with slotted spoon.

Add vermouth to the skillet over high heat and deglaze, scraping up brown bits from bottom. Add cream and rhubarb mixture, and cook 2 to 3 minutes. Serve over seafood. Serves 4.

Shrimp with Asparagus and Sesame Seeds

The rather smoky flavor of sesame seeds puts a fine edge on this spring stir-fry. Use a bland oil for frying so the flavor won't interfer.

1 1/2 lb	asparagus	750 g
1 tbsp	sesame seeds	15 mL
1/3 cup	vegetable oil	75 mL
3	green onions, sliced	3
1 1/2 lb	fresh shrimp, peeled	750 g
4 tsp	soya sauce	20 mL
1/2 tsp	salt	2 mL

Trim and wash asparagus and cut into 2 inch (5 cm) pieces. Heat a heavy skillet over medium heat and toast sesame seeds until golden. Remove seeds and set aside.

Heat oil in the skillet over medium-high heat. Add asparagus and onions, and stir-fry 1 minute. Add shrimp and stir-fry until vegetables are tender-crisp and shrimp is no longer translucent. Stir in sesame seeds, soya sauce and salt. Serves 4.

Chocolate Death

This may well be the world's richest, darkest chocolate ice cream. I've named it after a dessert I once ate during a weak moment in a Vancouver restaurant, having fallen into bad company. Dieters, read and weep. For chocolate lovers only!

8 oz	cream cheese	250 g
1 cup	granulated sugar	250 mL
1 cup	milk	250 mL
1 cup	cocoa powder	250 mL
1	large egg	1
2 tsp	vanilla	10 mL
2 cups	heavy cream	500 mL

Put cheese, sugar and milk in a food processor or blender and whiz briefly. Add cocoa, egg, vanilla and blend again. While the machine is running, add cream through the feed tube. As soon as mixture is smooth and uniform in color, pour into an ice-cream machine and freeze according to manufacturer's directions. Indulge. Serves 6 to 8.

Spicy Rhubarb Crumble

Here's an old-time dessert that everybody loves, especially with vanilla ice cream.

1 lb	rhubarb, cleaned and trimmed	500 g
3/4 cup	brown sugar, firmly packed	175 mL
1/2 tsp	cinnamon	2 mL
1/4 tsp	cloves, ground	1 mL
l/4 cup	orange juice	50 mL
1 cup	rolled oats	250 mL
1/3 cup	flour	75 mL
1/2 tsp	salt	2 mL
4 tbsp	butter, melted	60 mL

Preheat oven to 350 F (180 C). Cut rhubarb into 1 inch (2 cm) pieces.

In a large bowl, combine rhubarb with 1/4 cup (50 mL) brown sugar and 1/2 cinnamon and cloves. Add orange juice. Mix well.

Butter a shallow 1 qt (1 L) glass baking dish and arrange rhubarb mixture in bottom of the dish.

In a small bowl, combine rolled oats, flour, salt, remaining sugar, cinnamon and cloves, and mix well. Add melted butter and mix ingredients until crumbly. Spread mixture over rhubarb.

Bake 20 to 30 minutes, or until rhubarb is tender and topping is golden brown and crisp.

Serve with vanilla ice cream or whipped cream. Serves 6 to 8.

FAST TRACK MENU

Artichoke and Carrot Fritatta
Radish and Mushroom Salad
Fresh Strawberries and Cream

Fritatta is a handy thing–good hot, warm or cold, good for brunch, lunch or dinner. Serve with thick slices of well-buttered brown toast and this fast colorful salad. For dessert, elegant simplicity–strawberries and cream.

Artichoke and Carrot Fritatta

10 oz	pkg frozen artichoke hearts, thawed	284 g
8	eggs, beaten	8
1 cup	Cheddar cheese, grated	250 mL
1 cup	carrot, grated	250 mL
1/2 cup	parsley, finely chopped	125 mL
1	small onion, chopped	1
3	cloves garlic, pressed	3
1 tbsp	ketchup	15 mL
1 tsp	salt	5 mL
1/4 tsp	pepper	1 mL

Preheat oven to 300 F (150 C). Slice artichoke hearts into 2 or 3 pieces each. Combine remaining ingredients and blend well.

Pour into a lightly greased 9 inch (2 L) baking dish. Bake 20 to 30 minutes until golden brown. (Do not overbake.) Let fritatta sit 5 minutes before cutting.

Cut into squares and serve. Serves 4 generously.

Radish and Mushroom Salad

The first red radishes of spring are lovely to look at and they make an exquisite mouthful. They're also delicious with the slightly earthy flavor of mushrooms.

SALAD

2 cups	fresh mushrooms, thinly sliced	500 mL
2 cups	red radishes, thinly sliced	500 mL
8 to 12	romaine or butter lettuce leaves	8 to 12
1	egg, hard-cooked and sieved	1
1/4 cup	chives, chopped	50 mL

Place mushrooms and radishes in 2 separate bowls.

DRESSING

2 tbsp	lemon juice	30 mL
1/4 cup	vegetable oil	50 mL
1 tsp	egg, beaten	5 mL
1	small garlic clove, crushed	1
1/2 tsp	sugar	2 mL
dash	each, salt and pepper	dash
1/4 tsp	ground cumin	1 mL

In a blender, combine all ingredients. Process about 5 seconds, or until mixture is thick and creamy. Drizzle dressing equally over mushrooms and radishes and toss. Set aside. Arrange lettuce leaves on four salad plates. Drain mushrooms and radishes, reserving dressing. Mound mushrooms equally on centers of lettuce-lined plates. Arrange radishes around mushrooms on each plate. Sprinkle egg and chives equally over salads. Drizzle each salad with reserved dressing. Serves 4.

Fresh Strawberries and Cream

2 cups	fresh strawberries	500 mL
2 tbsp	dark brown sugar	30 mL
1/2 cup	cream, whipped	125 mL
1/2 cup	plain yogurt	125 mL

Hull and halve berries. Whip cream with sugar, then whip in yogurt. Serves 4.

CHAPTER 6
June

Summer in the Kitchen

June Recipes

There are things we eat in summer that will never taste so good again.

To stand in your own garden, knee-deep in dinner, with the corn waving and the dog demanding green peas (he knows what's good, this wily beast) and the zucchini getting fatter by the hour–this is a sweet moment.

Run these by your mental taste buds: A baby green bean just off the vine. A carrot so sweet it tastes sugared, a tomato that has ripened honestly in the sun. Marble-sized potatoes, steamed with butter and fresh dillweed. Baby beets cooked with their tops, swimming in butter with a dash of vinegar. And the first ear of corn snapping and squeaking when you pull off the husk, with the greener-than-grass smell tickling your nose.

Mortal food doesn't get much better.

The wonderful thing about summer food is that it requires so little of the cook. To complicate it with fancy sauces and excessive flavorings is to mess with perfection.

Green beans, for instance. What's to do? Wash them, snap off their tails, steam them until they're still crisp–bang, they're ready, and you won't find a better dish anywhere. Add salt and pepper if you wish, or butter (you can never have too much butter) and eat them just like that.

Better still, cook the whole garden–green and yellow beans, peas, tiny potatoes, small carrots with a bit of stem left on, cherry tomatoes, baby beets, cobs of corn.

Now steam each vegetable according to its needs. (This will vary. I like garden things barely cooked; others love 'em limp. There's no accounting for taste.)

Pile the corn in the middle of a giant platter and arrange the vegetables in mounds around them. Melt a lot of butter and pour it over the vegetables. Serve right away, with fresh chopped herbs, salt and extra butter on the side.

Iced Pear-Celery Soup

This unusual recipe came to me from a man who devised it while dieting. It's a perfect summer soup.

4 cups	celery, chopped	1 L
3 cups	chicken stock or broth	750 mL
2	pears, peeled and chopped	2
1/3 cup	dry white wine	75 mL
dash	cinnamon	dash
dash	salt	dash

Simmer celery in chicken stock, uncovered, about 15 minutes, or until soft. Drain and purée celery and pears in a food processor or blender a little at a time, adding hot broth in a thin stream. Empty into a mixing bowl and stir in wine and cinnamon. Cool to room temperature. Chill. Taste and correct seasoning with salt. Serves 4.

Peach Soup with White Port

White port and peaches make a beautiful combination. Serve this as a starter for a special brunch.

6	ripe peaches	6
1/4 cup	orange juice	50 mL
2 tbsp	white port	30 mL
2/3 cup	buttermilk	150 mL
1/2 tsp	cloves	2 mL
pinch	allspice	pinch
pinch	ginger	pinch

Peel peaches after immersing them in boiling water about 20 seconds. Chop coarsely and purée in batches in a food processor or blender. Stir in remaining ingredients and refrigerate. Serve ice-cold. Serves 4.

Pasta Chicken Salad with Apricot-Basil Dressing

Buy a cooked chicken breast at the deli on the way home from work. It makes this salad almost a whole meal.

SALAD

1 cup	fusilli (corkscrew) pasta	250 mL
1 tsp	salad oil	5 mL
6	fresh ripe apricots, cut into quarters	6
1	chicken breast, boned, skinned, cooked and shredded	1
2	small zucchini, cut into julienne	2
1	red bell pepper, cut into julienne	1
3 tbsp	fresh basil, chopped **OR**	45 mL
1 tbsp	dry basil	15 mL
	fresh apricot-basil dressing	

Cook pasta in boiling water 10 to 12 minutes or as package directs. Drain, toss with salad oil and let cool. Combine pasta, apricots, chicken, zucchini, red pepper and basil in a bowl. Pour fresh apricot-basil dressing over. Toss gently. Serves 4.

DRESSING

2	fresh ripe apricots, pitted	2
2 tbsp	white wine vinegar	30 mL
1 tbsp	sugar	15 mL
1/4 cup	vegetable oil	50 mL
1 tbsp	fresh basil **OR**	15 mL
1 tsp	dry basil	5 mL

Combine apricots, vinegar and sugar in a blender. Purée until smooth. Continue blending while slowly adding vegetable oil. When thick and smooth, stir in basil. Makes 1 cup (250 mL).

Summer Couscous

During one memorable stay in an apartment on the Ile de la Cite in Paris, I developed a passion for this salad, which came from a fancy food shop around the corner. The woman who owned the shop refused to part with the recipe, so I took the last batch apart, grain by grain. I think I've got it.

SALAD

2 cups	boiling water	500 mL
1 tsp	chicken granules	5 mL
1 tbsp	olive oil	15 mL
1 cup	quick-cooking couscous	250 mL
1	green onion, chopped	1
3 or 4	radishes, finely diced	3 or 4
1/2 cup	tiny peas	125 mL
1/2	sweet red pepper, finely diced	1/2
1 tbsp	fresh mint, chopped	15 mL
1/4 cup	fresh parsley, chopped	50 mL

DRESSING

	juice of 1 lemon	
2 tbsp	red wine vinegar	30 mL
1/2 tsp	ground ginger	2 mL
	salt and pepper to taste	
1/2 cup	olive oil	125 mL

Dissolve chicken granules in boiling water. Add olive oil. Pour in couscous, stirring rapidly so it doesn't lump. Remove from heat and cover. Let stand 5 minutes.

Remove cover and fluff with a fork, repeating several times to break up lumps as couscous cools.

Prepare vegetables and add to cooled couscous, tossing to mix. If using frozen peas, place under cold running water to defrost–there's no need to cook them.

Put dressing ingredients in a screw-cap jar and shake. Pour over couscous. Toss to distribute evenly. Taste for seasoning. Refrigerate up to 8 hours.

Serve with grilled meat of any kind, especially lamb. Serves 4.

Indian Eggplant Salad with Garlic

Here's a flexible dish for days when you find fat purple eggplant and ripe tomatoes in the market. I love to play with the flavors–a dash of cinnamon, an extra clove of garlic, more curry powder. Just keep tasting until you get it right. Serve cold with warm pita bread or as a relish to accompany barbecued meat.

1	large eggplant, cubed	1
4 tbsp	salad oil	60 mL
2 to 4	cloves garlic, minced	2 to 4
1	onion, diced	1
2	stalks celery, diced	2
1	fresh jalapeño pepper, minced	1
1	green pepper, diced	1
1	red pepper, diced	1
4	ripe tomatoes, peeled	4
4 tbsp	tomato sauce	60 mL
1 tbsp	sugar	15 mL
2 tbsp	wine vinegar	30 mL
1 tsp	cinnamon	5 mL
1 tsp	oregano	5 mL
2 tsp	curry powder	10 mL
	salt and pepper to taste	

Pour olive oil into a Dutch oven. Sauté eggplant and garlic, taking care not to burn. Add other vegetables and tomato sauce, sugar, vinegar and seasonings. Stir. Cover and turn heat to low. Simmer vegetables 30 minutes, stirring and tasting often.

When vegetables are barely tender, pour in batches into a food processor or blender and process until coarsely chopped. Pour into a large glass container and chill. Keeps approximately 1 week in the refrigerator. Serves 6 to 8.

Thai Salad with Rose Petals

This salad is positively seductive. If you don't have roses, use nasturtiums, marigold or pansy petals, providing they haven't been sprayed with herbicides. Rice sticks are available in any oriental market–they puff up instantly when they hit hot oil.

3	dark roses, petals only	3
3 cups	chicken, cooked and shredded	750 mL
1 1/2 tbsp	hoisin sauce	22 mL
1/2 cup	green onion tops, shredded	125 mL
1/2 tsp	sesame seed oil	2 mL
2 tbsp	lemon juice	30 mL
3 tbsp	peanuts, finely chopped	45 mL
3 tbsp	sesame seeds, toasted	45 mL
l/4 lb	fine rice sticks, broken	125 g
2 cups	iceberg lettuce, shredded	500 mL

Cut petals of 2 roses into long, thin strands and combine with chicken, hoisin sauce, green onion, sesame seed oil, lemon juice and 2 tbsp (30 mL) each, peanuts and sesame seeds. Toss to mix well and set aside.

Fry rice sticks in hot oil, a few at a time, until just golden. Drain on paper towels.

Toss 2/3 rice sticks with chicken mixture and arrange on a bed of shredded lettuce. Top with remaining rice sticks, peanuts and sesame seeds. Shred petals of last rose over salad. Serves 8.

Grilled Vegetables with Yogurt Salad

Grilled vegetables develop a smokey-sweet flavor. These make a terrific first course or can be served with any barbecued meat.

VEGETABLES

2	Japanese eggplants, sliced lengthwise	2
1	large red onion, cut into thick slices	1
2	zucchini, sliced lengthwise	2
1	red bell pepper, quartered and seeded	1
1	green bell pepper, quartered and seeded	1
4	extra large mushrooms	4

MARINADE

1 cup	extra virgin olive oil	250 mL
1/3 cup	balsamic vinegar	75 mL
2 tbsp	fresh rosemary, chopped	30 mL
1 tbsp	garlic, minced	15 mL

Combine all ingredients for marinade. Marinate vegetables 1 hour. Gently grill vegetables over coals until soft, brushing often with marinade. Arrange on a platter and serve hot or at room temperature with yogurt salad. Serves 4.

YOGURT SALAD

1 cup	plain yogurt	250 mL
1	cucumber, peeled and chopped	1
2	cloves garlic, finely minced	2
2 tbsp	green onion, chopped	30 mL
1 tbsp	fresh dill, chopped	15 mL

Combine ingredients and refrigerate overnight before using. Use as a dressing for grilled vegetables.

Fresh Corn Fritters

These are raggedy around the edges, like edible doilies. The flavor is unbearably delicious.

10	ears of corn	10
3	eggs	3
1 tbsp	flour	15 mL
1 tsp	salt	5 mL
3 tbsp	butter	45 mL
1 tbsp	corn oil	15 mL

Grate corn into a large bowl. Separate eggs and beat whites until stiff. Mix yolks into corn, along with flour and salt. Gently fold whites into mixture.

Heat butter and oil in a skillet and fry little blobs of batter as you would pancakes, turning once. Serve hot with corn syrup (to which is added a few drops of molasses). Serves 6 to 8.

Fresh Tomato-Mozzarella Sauce

This is one of the simplest and best cool sauces for pasta. The mozzarella cubes give it a chewy, meaty texture.

3	large ripe tomatoes, peeled and chopped	3
2 to 3 tbsp	fresh basil, minced	30 to 45 mL
1	large clove garlic, minced	1
	pepper to taste	
3/4 cup	mozzarella cheese, cubed	175 mL

Combine everything in a glass or ceramic bowl and let flavors blend for about 1 hour. Serve at room temperature over hot pasta. Makes enough for about 1 1/2 cups (375 mL) of pasta.

Hot Hot Barbecue Sauce

For my money, this is possibly the world's best barbecue sauce. It came to me from a Hong Kong chef, who got it from his sister in California. It needs a food processor or a lot of hand chopping.

2	onions	2
3	garlic cloves	3
1	large lemon	1
1 lb	blue plums	500 g
1 cup	dried apricots	250 mL
3 tbsp	fresh ginger, chopped	45 mL
1/2 cup	white vinegar	125 mL
1/2 cup	cider vinegar	125 mL
1/2 cup	sweet sherry	125 mL
1 cup	brown sugar	250 mL
1/2 cup	molasses	125 mL
1/2 tsp	ground cloves	2 mL
1 1/2 tsp	cinnamon	7 mL
2	dry chili peppers, crushed	2
dash	Tabasco sauce	dash
1 tsp	salt	5 mL
1/4 cup	cilantro, chopped	50 mL

Roughly chop onion, garlic and fruit. In a food processor process onion, garlic, lemon, plums and apricots. Add remaining ingredients, except cilantro, and process until puréed.

Pour into a large pot and bring to boil. Lower heat. Simmer until thickened, about 40 minutes, stirring often to avoid burning. Remove from heat and let cool. Add cilantro. Taste for seasoning. Pour into a 1 qt (1 L) jar and refrigerate. Will keep 1 month. Makes 4 cups (1 L).

Salmon Yakitori with Peaches

Serve yakitori salmon with steamed rice and stir-fried snow peas.

SALMON

1 lb	salmon filet, cut into 16 large cubes	500 g
2	fresh peaches, each cut into 8 wedges	2
2	medium zucchini	2
1	sweet red pepper, cut into squares	1
	yakitori sauce	

Cut zucchini into l inch (2 cm) diagonal slices (use a crinkle cutter if you have one).

Alternate salmon, peach, zucchini and pepper on 8 long metal skewers. Place in a shallow baking pan and pour yakitori sauce over top. Marinate in refrigerator 2 to 3 hours. Grill 4 inches (10 cm) above hot coals, turning once, 5 to 6 minutes per side. Brush with remaining yakitori sauce while cooking. Serves 4.

YAKITORI SAUCE

l/2 cup	water	125 mL
1/4 cup	soya sauce	50 mL
1/4 cup	sherry	50 mL
3 tbsp	sugar	45 mL
1 tsp	ginger root, grated	5 mL

Combine all ingredients in a saucepan. Cook over medium-high heat, stirring constantly, until mixture comes to boil and thickens. Makes about 1 cup (250 mL).

Scented Geranium and Apple Sorbet

I first ate this between courses at Sooke Harbor House, a restaurant on Vancouver Island that is justly famous for its inventive cuisine.

1	apple, peeled, cored and sliced	1
1 cup	dry, hard apple cider	250 mL
1 tsp	lemon juice	5 mL
2 tbsp	scented geranium leaves, finely chopped (preferably Rose, Silver Leaf Rose, Prince Rupert or Lemon varieties)	30 mL

Heat apple and cider in a medium saucepan. Cook until apple is tender. Add lemon juice and remove from heat. Let cool. Add scented geranium leaves. Process in an ice cream machine, following manufacturer's directions. Serves 4.

Peach Ice Cream

A simple ice cream, but delicious. Serve with fresh peach sauce–peaches puréed in a blender and sweetened with a dash of peach brandy or amaretto liqueur.

3	ripe peaches, peeled and chopped	3
2/3 cup	sugar	150 mL
4 tsp	lemon juice	20 mL
1 cup	whole milk	250 ml
1 cup	whipping cream	250 ml
2	egg yolks	2

Mix together chopped peaches, 1/3 cup (75 mL) sugar and lemon juice. Set aside. Combine milk, cream, egg yolks and remaining 1/3 cup (75 mL) sugar in a saucepan. Cook over medium heat, stirring constantly, until it begins to bubble, about 3 or 4 minutes. Stir in peach mixture. Cool.

Pour into an ice cream machine and freeze according to manufacturer's directions. Makes about 5 cups (1.25 L).

Fresh Plum Lattice Pie

From a Hutterite woman at a farmers' market comes this traditional plum pie.

16	fresh plums	16
1 1/2 cups	sugar	375 mL
1/3 cup	cornstarch	75 mL
1/2 tsp	fresh ginger, grated	2 mL
1/4 tsp	salt	1 mL
1 tbsp	butter	15 mL
1 tsp	orange peel	5 mL
1 tbsp	orange juice	15 mL
9 inch	pastry for double-crust pie	22 cm

Preheat oven to 425 F (220 C). Quarter and pit 13 plums. (Reserve 3.) In a large saucepan, combine plums, sugar, cornstarch, ginger, salt, butter, orange peel and juice. Heat, stirring, until sugar liquefies, about 8 minutes. Set aside to cool slightly.

Roll out generous 1/2 pastry on a lightly floured surface. Line a 9 inch (23 cm) pie plate with high edge. Roll out remaining pastry on a lightly floured surface and cut into strips for lattice top.

Pour plum mixture into pastry-lined pie plate. Cut remaining plums into quarters and lay skin-side down over plum mixture. Place strips in lattice pattern on top of pie. Crimp and seal edges.

Bake 10 minutes. Reduce temperature to 350 F (180 C) and continue baking 40 minutes more. Let cool before serving. Serves 6 to 8.

Nectarine Mousse Pie

This pie is as light as a cloud and has great flavor. To speed things up, use a frozen pie shell.

9 inch	prepared pie shell	22 cm
1	envelope plain gelatin	1
3/4 cup	granulated sugar	175 mL
3/4 cup	cold water	175 ml
3	large eggs	3
3 tbsp	dark rum	45 mL
2	large fresh nectarines, puréed	2
1 cup	whipping cream	250 mL
2	nectarines for decoration, sliced	2
	lemon juice for dipping	

Bake pie shell according to instructions. Cool.

Combine gelatin and sugar in a saucepan, and mix well. Stir in water and let stand 5 minutes. Dissolve over low heat, stirring constantly. Beat eggs lightly. Stir a little gelatin mixture into eggs. Combine with remaining gelatin, stirring constantly over low heat until custard thickens slightly, about 5 minutes.

Remove from heat and stir in rum and puréed nectarines. Cool until mixture begins to thicken and set.

Beat cream to soft peaks. Fold cream into gelatin mixture. Chill until mixture mounds on a spoon. Heap into pie shell. Chill several hours or overnight. Decorate with additional sliced nectarines just before serving. (Dip nectarine slices in lemon juice to prevent browning.) Serves 6 to 8.

FAST TRACK MENU

Spaghetti with Zucchini
Fresh Fruit Broil

Easy, easy, easy–and so good. Use the best extra virgin olive oil for maximum flavor.
Serve with a glass of chianti.

Spaghetti with Zucchini

10 oz	thin spaghetti	300 g
3	zucchini, thinly sliced into rounds	3
1/3 cup	olive oil	75 mL
	salt and pepper to taste	
6	fresh basil leaves, finely chopped	6
1 cup	fresh Parmesan cheese, grated	250 mL

Sauté zucchini in 2 tbsp (30 mL) oil over high heat 8 to 10 minutes. Add salt and
pepper.

Cook spaghetti 7 minutes in plenty of rapidly boiling salted water. Drain. Add
zucchini with cooking juices to remainding oil and basil. Season with pepper. Mix
well. Serve hot, tossed with grated cheese. Serves 4.

Fresh Fruit Broil

2	peaches, halved	2
2	bananas, halved	2
4 tsp	banana sugar	20 mL
4	scoops vanilla ice cream	4

Preheat the broiler. Place fruit in a broiler pan. Sprinkle with sugar. Broil 4 inches
(10 cm) from the element until sugar bubbles. Serve with ice cream. Serves 4.

CHAPTER 7
July

Y'All Come!

July Recipes

"After a good dinner I can forgive anyone, even my own relations."–Oscar Wilde

Of all the parties in the world, the family reunion takes the cake for human comedy, melodrama and overeating. Summer is its finest season.

No sooner does summer vacation dawn than our nation's highways clog with out-of-province cars, each one stuffed with children, pets and food. Airport departure lounges look like Sunday at the zoo, and you can't get a flight for love nor money. Everyone's heading home for dinner.

Ah, those dinners. Oscar Wilde wasn't the only one who had mixed emotions about family feasts. A friend of mine refers to his yearly summer pilgrimage back to Saskatchewan as "The Annual Bugtussle." But he hasn't missed one in 10 years.

THE PRELIMINARY ROUND

For the lucky host family, reunions are a time of loaves and fishes. Of adding another cup of water to the soup and then quadrupling the recipe. Of finding extra beds and extra chairs and enough cutlery to go around.

As the masses descend and the crowd in the kitchen grows, there's the introduction of new spouses, offspring and live-in companions ("This is my...er...friend"). And there's the silent totting up of loss and gain since the last reunion.

"Getting a little thin on top, eh, Portnoy? Didn't recognize you without hair!" (Big laugh from the assembled relatives; Portnoy grins and bears it.)

For the kids, obligatory cheek-kissing and head-patting must be endured. "Is this really little Portia? My, isn't she tall! And look at those braces!" (This, to a child who threatens to wear a brick on her head if she grows another centimeter, and has refused to smile since the last visit to the orthodontist.)

And so it goes.

THE MAIN EVENT

Though the average reunion is a process of constant eating, there is generally one feast that outshines all others. It's the one for which we get dressed up, speak firmly to dogs and children and resolve to behave ourselves no matter what.

It's also the one with the best food. Grandma trots out her own private recipe for fried chicken. The barbecued roast smells so good that people keep traipsing by just to sniff. There's coleslaw with celery seeds, the wobbly jellied salads you haven't seen since the last reunion and a pale dish known as "Aunt Cissie's Dump Salad" puts miniature marshmallows back on the map. (As one astute observer of the human scene once noted,, "We snicker, but we lick the bowl.") And of course there's peach shortcake.

No sooner are tables set on the lawn than clouds roll in, the first raindrop splatters on the tablecloth and the whole affair has to be moved inside. So doth the cookie crumble.

But eventually everybody is seated somewhere, and there's a long-winded grace by a pious uncle, during which Portnoy Jr. spills his milk.

THE AFTERMATH

The last chicken bone has been chewed and the teapot's been around twice. All the women will now go, willy-nilly, to the kitchen to mop hundreds of dishes because Grandma still doesn't have a dishwasher. Initially, a few will hang back–new spouses or companions who don't know the routine, and those sophisticates wearing $50 worth of silk-wrap from Nails 'n' Lashes. The senior aunts jockey for position around the sink, and those with political clout get to wash. Everybody else dries, making sudden, determined forays into the mob around the sink, grabbing a plate and polishing madly with a soaking-wet dishtowel.

Meanwhile, the men sit around, digesting. They're everywhere–under trees, in the basement, in the living room. Everywhere, that is, except the kitchen.

The younger children scrap and howl and twiddle any dials they can find. The older ones go into a huddle behind the garage, smoking illicit cigarettes, lying about their social lives and generally being cool. The dog, who helped himself to most of Aunt Petunia's hamburger casserole and licked several platters clean, naps in a corner. Later, he will be sick on Grandma's carpet.

And they'll all be back again next year.

Dump Salad

The Fifties were the heyday of the miniature marshmallow, and they were never more snootily presented than in this salad, which was also known as Wedding Salad. It has been showing up at family gatherings ever since, and there are seldom leftovers.

2 cups	shredded coconut	500 mL
2 cups	mandarin oranges, drained	500 mL
2 cups	crushed pineapple, drained	500 mL
2 cups	sour cream	500 mL
2 cups	miniature marshmallows (white only!)	500 mL

Fold all ingredients together in a large bowl. Cover with plastic and chill a few hours or overnight to allow flavors to blend. Fold again just before serving. Serves 12.

Tortellini Vegetable Salad

Buy frozen cheese tortellini to make this salad and double the recipe for a crowd.

1 1/2 cups	mayonnaise	375 mL
1 tsp	dry mustard	5 mL
1 cup	fresh basil, chopped	250 mL
1 cup	fresh parsley, chopped	250 mL
1/4 cup	milk	50 mL
2	cloves garlic, minced	2
2	carrots, julienne	2
2	zucchini, julienne	2
2	green onions, chopped	2
20	cherry tomatoes, halved	20
4 cups	cheese tortellini, cooked	1 L
	salt and pepper to taste	
1/2 cup	pine nuts (optional)	125 mL

Combine mayonnaise, mustard, herbs, milk and garlic. Mix well. Add remaining ingredients, folding in tortellini at the last so it doesn't break up. Chill at least 1 hour for flavor to mellow. If desired, fold in pine nuts before serving. Serves 8.

Celery Seed Coleslaw

Whether you serve this big batch salad to a crowd or keep it for a week of smaller meals, it's a handy dish.

1 cup	cider vinegar	250 mL
1 cup	sugar	250 mL
1 tsp	caraway seeds	5 mL
2 tsp	celery seeds	10 mL
1 tsp	turmeric	5 mL
2 tsp	salt	10 mL
1/2 cup	salad oil	125 mL
1/3 cup	water	75 mL
1 Ib	fresh green beans	500 g
3 lb	cabbage, finely shredded	1.5 kg
2	onions, diced	2
2	carrots, grated	2

Place vinegar, sugar, caraway seeds, celery seeds, turmeric, salt, salad oil and water in a saucepan. Bring to boil. When sugar has dissolved, remove from heat and let cool.

Cut beans into 1/2 inch (1 cm) lengths and cook in salted water about 5 minutes, until just barely tender. Drain and rinse under cool water.

Combine cabbage, onion, carrot and beans. Add dressing and toss to mix. Cover tightly and refrigerate overnight before serving. Keeps 1 week in the refrigerator. Serves 16.

Beef on a Spit

This party-sized barbecue is perfect for a summer crowd.

8	garlic cloves	8
12 lb	rolled prime rib of beef	7 kg
1/3 cup	butter, softened	75 mL
2 tbsp	black pepper, coarsely ground	30 mL
2 tbsp	grainy mustard	30 mL

Cut garlic into slivers. Make a few slits in fat and insert 1/2 garlic. Insert remaining garlic into roast between meat and fat and push barbecue spit through center of roast, testing to see that it's well balanced.

In a small dish, stir soft butter, pepper and mustard together, and spread about half on roast. Insert meat thermometer into thick part of roast.

Arrange a drip pan in the barbecue. Roast beef over medium-hot coals about 4 hours, until it reaches 140 F (60 C) for rare, 145 F (65 C) for medium. Baste twice. Let roast stand 10 to 15 minutes for juices to set. Serves 10 to 12.

Landers' Loaf

Eons ago, Ann Landers ran a meatloaf recipe in her column. She's still getting requests for repeats.

2 lbs	ground beef, lean	1 kg
2	eggs, beaten	2
1 1/2 cups	bread crumbs	375 mL
3/4 cup	ketchup	175 mL
1 tsp	Accent	5 mL
1/2 cup	warm water	125 mL
1 1/2 oz	pkg dry onion soup mix	45 g
1 tsp	salt	5 mL
1/2 tsp	pepper	2 mL
2	bacon strips	2
1 cup	tomato sauce	250 mL

Preheat oven to 350 F (180 C). Mix together all ingredients except tomato sauce and bacon. Pat mixture into a 9 x 5 inch (2 L) oiled loaf pan. Lay bacon strips the length of the loaf and pour sauce over top. Bake 1 hour. Let rest 10 minutes before slicing. Serves 6.

Barley Pilaf with Fruit and Nuts

Barley has great texture, and when you mix it with fruit and nuts it's almost a whole meal. Delicious.

2 cups	pearl barley	500 mL
1/2 cup	butter	125 mL
1 1/2 cups	slivered almonds	375 mL
2	onions, chopped	2
1	apple, cored and chopped	1
1	celery stalk, chopped	1
1 cup	fresh parsley, chopped	250 mL
1 tsp	salt	5 mL
1 tsp	pepper	5 mL
5 cups	chicken stock	1.25 mL
2 cups	apple juice	500 mL

Preheat oven to 350 F (180 C). Rinse barley and drain well. In a frypan, melt 1/2 butter over medium heat. Add almonds and brown, stirring constantly. Remove with slotted spoon. Add remaining butter to skillet, then add onions, apple, celery and barley. Stir-fry until onions are soft.

Pour into a 4 qt (4 L) casserole. Add salt and pepper. Heat stock and juice to boiling and pour into barley mixture. Bake, covered, 1 hour, or until barley is tender. Stir occasionally, adding a little water if casserole seems dry. Serves 12 to 14.

Saskatoon Pie

9 inch	pie shell	22 cm
1 qt	saskatoons	1 L
1 tbsp	flour	15 mL
3/4 cup	sugar	175 mL
1/2 cup	cream	125 mL

Pat pastry into pie plate.

In a large bowl, toss saskatoons, flour, sugar and cream. Pour into pastry shell. Top with crust and pinch edges together. Cut slits in pastry. Bake at 375 F (190 C) 15 minutes. Reduce heat to 350 F (180 C) and continue baking until juices bubble and crust is golden. Serves 6 generously.

Note: If saskatoons are unavailable, blueberries may be substituted.

Fresh Peach Shortcake

The peach schnapps in the filling is optional, but it's a lovely touch. If you'd rather have strawberry or blueberry shortcake, just substitute the fruit. Or make all three and knock 'em dead.

SHORTCAKE

3 cups	flour, sifted	750 mL
4 1/2 tsp	baking powder	22 mL
3 tbsp	sugar	45 mL
1 1/2 tsp	salt	7 mL
3/4 cup	shortening	175 mL
1	egg, beaten	1
1 cup	milk	250 mL

Preheat oven to 450 F (230 C). Grease a 9 inch (2 L) layer cake pan. Sift dry ingredients together. Cut shortening in by hand or with the metal blade in a food processor.

Add egg and gradually add milk, stirring with a fork until just blended and dough forms a ball. (You may not need all the milk.) Dough should be soft.

Pat dough into the greased pan. Bake 25 to 30 minutes, until golden brown. Remove from oven and turn out onto a wire rack to cool. When cool, cut in half horizontally.

FILLING

8	ripe peaches, peeled and sliced	8
1/4 cup	peach schnapps	50 mL
1/2 cup	sugar	125 mL
1 cup	cream, whipped	250 mL

Sprinkle peaches with sugar. Place bottom layer of shortcake on a serving plate and cover with 1/2 peaches, drizzling 1/2 schnapps over top. Cover second layer of shortcake with a few more peaches and remaining schnapps, then slather whipped cream over top and garnish with remaining peaches. For a smashing presentation, tuck a few green leaves (berry, peach, even apple) around the edge of the plate. Serves 6.

Squash Pie with Maple Cream

My aunt Bernice had 7 children and the best reunions were always at her house. Squash pie appears in our family cookbook under her name. If you aren't a squash grower, use canned pumpkin.

PIE
9 inch	unbaked pie crust	22 cm
3	eggs, well beaten	3
3/4 cup	brown sugar	175 mL
1 tsp	salt	5 mL
1 tsp	cinnamon	5 mL
1/2 tsp	nutmeg	2 mL
1/2 tsp	allspice	2 mL
1 tsp	ground ginger	5 mL
2 cups	evaporated milk	500 mL
2 cups	cooked yellow squash, mashed	500 mL

Preheat oven to 450 F (230 C). Beat eggs, sugar, salt and spices together. Gradually beat in evaporated milk, then add mashed squash, straining first if stringy. Pour into pie shell. Bake 10 minutes, then reduce heat to 325 F(160 C) and continue baking 30 minutes more, or until firm. Cool pie. Just before serving, top with whipped maple cream. Serves 6.

TOPPING
1 cup	whipping cream	250 mL
1/4 cup	maple syrup	50 mL

Whip cream until stiff. Pour maple syrup in a fine stream over cream, folding it in. Swirl over top of pie.

Maple Chocolate Paté

This may be the world's easiest dessert, and after a big meal it's just right. Forks aren't necessary—just plates, small knives, fresh fruit and good, plain cookies such as shortbread, wheatmeal or coffee biscuits.

2 cups	semisweet chocolate chips	500 mL
1 3/4 cups	whipping cream	425 mL
5 tbsp	unsalted butter	75 mL
1 tsp	maple flavoring	5 mL
1 cup	walnuts, chopped (optional)	250 mL
	cookies, strawberries and papaya chunks	

The day before: Melt chocolate in a double boiler. Heat cream until scalded, stirring constantly. Remove cream from heat and add melted chocolate, butter and maple flavoring, stirring to help thicken slightly.

Spoon chocolate paté into an attractive dish or crock, and cover tightly with plastic wrap. Refrigerate overnight.

To serve, bring paté out of the refrigerator 1 hour ahead of time. Stir with a fork. If very stiff, add a little warmed cream. If using walnuts, stir them in now. (I've tried adding them when I make the paté, but they get soggy.)

Guests spread paté on biscuits and eat with fresh fruit.

Peanut Fudge Ice Cream

On a hot July afternoon, this soft creamy homemade peanut fudge ice cream is my idea of heaven.

1 cup	semisweet chocolate chips	250 mL
2 cups	milk	500 mL
1 cup	sugar	250 mL
2/3 cup	peanut butter	150 mL
2 tsp	vanilla extract	10 mL
2 cups	whipping cream	500 mL
3/4 cup	Spanish peanuts	175 mL

Melt chocolate chips over hot water. Stir in milk, sugar and peanut butter. Cool to room temperature. Stir in vanilla and whipping cream. Pour into an ice cream maker and freeze according to manufacturer's directions. Makes 2 qt (2 L).

FAST TRACK MENU

Oven Barbecued Ribs with Sweet-and-Sour Sauce
Chutney Baked Beans
Greens with Sweet Tarragon Dressing
Beer 'n' Mozza Bread
Ice Cream Sundaes

Unexpected company comes in large numbers. Here's a fast way to feed a crowd.

Oven Barbecued Ribs with Sweet-and-Sour Sauce

These are oven-barbecued to save trouble for the cook.

RIBS

8 lb	pork back ribs	4 kg
3 cups	water	750 mL
1/2 cup	soya sauce	125 mL
1 tbsp	cornstarch	15 mL
2 cups	sweet-and-sour sauce	500 mL

Preheat oven to 350 F (180 C). Place pork back ribs in a Dutch oven. Add water. Bring to boil and reduce heat. Cover and simmer 10 minutes. Remove ribs and drain.

Mix soya sauce and cornstarch. Brush on both sides of ribs. Place in a large roaster. Cover and bake until meat pulls easily from bone, about 45 minutes. Drizzle with sauce and baste every 10 minutes. Remove cover for last 10 minutes of baking time. Cut into serving pieces. Serves 10 to 12.

SAUCE

1 cup	water	250 mL
1/2 cup	ketchup	125 mL
1/4 cup	HP or steak sauce	50 mL
1/4 cup	molasses	50 mL
1/4 cup	vinegar	50 mL
1 tbsp	chili powder	15 mL

Mix and heat all ingredients to boiling. Remove from heat and drizzle on ribs. Makes about 2 cups (500 mL).

Chutney Baked Beans

I use plum chutney for this, but peach, mango or Major Grey are equally good. If you stir them together the night before, they'll taste even better, and the leftovers are delicious.

1 cup	fruit chutney	250 mL
1	small onion, diced	1
1/4 cup	molasses	50 mL
28 oz	can baked beans	795 mL

Preheat oven to 350 F (180 C). Stir all ingredients together in a 1 1/2 qt (1.5 L) bean pot. Bake, covered, 50 minutes (while the Beer 'n' Mozza Bread bakes). Remove cover, stir beans and bake 10 minutes more. Serves 10 to 12.

Greens with Sweet Tarragon Dressing

DRESSING

1/4 cup	canola oil	50 mL
1/4 cup	white vinegar	50 mL
1 tsp	orange peel, finely grated	5 mL
1 tsp	dried tarragon	5 mL
2 tbsp	honey	30 mL
1/2 tsp	salt	2 mL
	juice of 1 orange	

Put all ingredients in a blender and run on high until thick and creamy. Store, covered, in the refrigerator. Makes just over 1 cup (250 mL).

SALAD

1	head romaine lettuce, torn	1
1	head iceberg lettuce, torn	1
1	orange, peeled and sliced	1
2	green onions, sliced	2

Put torn lettuce into a large bowl. Peel and slice orange, cutting each slice into quarters. Add green onion. Drizzle dressing over top and toss just before serving. Serves 10 to 12.

Beer 'n' Mozza Bread

There are endless variations of beer bread making the rounds, but this one, adapted from good cook Sheila Devereux, is my favorite. When it's hot it has a texture close to yeast bread and a nice yeasty flavor. Cheddar cheese may be used instead of mozzarella.

1 3/4 cups	beer	425 mL
2 1/2 cups	all-purpose flour	625 mL
4 tsp	baking powder	20 mL
1 tbsp	sugar	15 mL
1/2 tsp	salt	2 mL
1/2 tsp	white mustard seed	2 mL
1	green onion, finely chopped	1
1 cup	mozzarella cheese, grated	250 mL

Preheat oven to 350 F (180 C). Open beer and let sit at room temperature while greasing a 9 inch (2 L) loaf pan.

Mix all dry ingredients, including onion and cheese, in a large bowl. Pour in beer and stir just enough to combine well. Bake about 50 minutes, or until it passes the toothpick test. Cool 10 minutes. Serve warm, in thick slices, with plenty of butter. Makes 1 loaf.

Ice Cream Sundaes

Offer 3 flavors of ice cream and assorted toppings: nuts, fresh sliced fruit, chocolate syrup. Let everyone be creative.

CHAPTER 8
August

The Flavor of Life

August Recipes

"Market and religion. These alone bring men, unarmed, together since time began–To buy, to sell, to barter–To exchange, above all, human contact." –D.H. Lawrence, Mornings in Mexico

Since man began to plow the earth and plant seeds, farmers' markets have been a magnet for writers, artists and good cooks.

D. H. Lawrence loved the sound and fury of the Mexican farmers' markets, the violent bidding over garlic and corn. There was a passion for life in the market–music, color, an edible vitality that he cherished.

Years later, M.F.K. Fisher wrote about the markets of southern France. Even when she was alone, without kin or kitchen, she haunted the markets of Aix and Marseille, impetuously buying a tomato here, a bunch of flowers there. Brisked up by the human contact among the cabbages, she felt better.

Like most food lovers, I'm a market junkie. As a child, visiting Ontario aunts, the Kitchener Market thrilled me. In Vancouver, Granville Island Market was a powerful lure; it still is. The first thing I look for in any foreign city–Florence, Nice, Belgrade–is the street market, where I can see real people and smell and taste real food.

The first one I spent any time in was the old City Market in Edmonton, located in a vast, echoing hall, complete with an enormous, shedding moose head. On Saturday mornings the place was noisy and damp, and a wonderful aroma rose from the piles of vegetables, the home baking, the cheeses, even from recently-dispatched chickens.

At the time I had no kitchen, not even a hotplate, but who could resist the fat little beets, the bunches of basil and dill? I hung over the mountains of fresh carrots, sniffing something I'd been missing for months–the fresh, earthy smell that belonged exclusively to a carrot so recently pulled from the earth its top was still perky. I lugged my purchases around the stalls all morning, wondering what a woman with no kitchen could do with a bag of carrots, two pounds of baby beets and a fresh chicken.

Market people care deeply about what goes on their tables and into their mouths, and they're the same all over the world. If my favorite radish vendor from the Old Strathcona Market were suddenly transported, table and all, to the big morning markets in Nice or Aix, she'd hardly miss a beat. True, there might be some confusion at first while she converted loonies to francs, but with a certain amount of arm waving the bargain would be sealed, the radishes sold.

That's the great thing about farmers' markets–the vendors all speak a sort of gastronomic Esperanto. They can tell you how to roast a chicken or make a pickle, and they're generous with their recipes. The ones in this chapter have come from a variety of vendors, cooks and customers in markets from all around the world. Enjoy.

Baked Goat Cheese with Chutney Vinaigrette

Farmers' markets are often your best bet for fresh goat cheese. For this dish, buy the small round ones that have not been aged.

CHEESE

2 tbsp	olive oil	30 mL
1/2 cup	bread crumbs	125 mL
4	small goat cheeses	4
1	bunch spinach leaves, washed and dried	1
1	romaine lettuce heart, torn into 1 inch 2 (cm) pieces	1

Preheat oven to 475 F (240 C). Spoon olive oil into one bowl and bread crumbs into another.

Cut cheese into 4 wedges. Dip into olive oil, then roll in bread crumbs. Place in a shallow baking dish. Chill 15 minutes, then put into the oven and bake about 10 minutes, or until golden brown.

Meanwhile arrange a few spinach leaves on salad plates. Toss remaining spinach with romaine and place in center of each plate. Spoon 1 tbsp (15 mL) chutney vinaigrette over greens. Place warm goat cheese on top and spoon additional chutney vinaigrette over. Serve immediately. Serves 4 as an appetizer salad.

VINAIGRETTE

2 tbsp	red wine vinegar	30 mL
2 tbsp	mango chutney, chopped	30 mL
4 tbsp	salad oil	60 mL
1/2 tsp	salt	2 mL

Mix all ingredients together in a screw-cap jar and shake vigorously.

Cucumber and Strawberry Salad

English cucumbers and strawberries are always a favorite part of the market scene.

1/2	English cucumber, unpeeled	1/2
2 cups	strawberries, rinsed and hulled	500 mL
1 tsp	balsamic vinegar	5 mL
1 tbsp	lemon juice, freshly squeezed	15 mL
1/2 tsp	ginger, freshly grated	2 mL
1/4 tsp	salt	1 mL
4	leaves romaine lettuce	4

Cut cucumber lengthwise into quarters. Cut cucumber sections and strawberries in thin slices. Whisk together lemon juice, ginger and salt. Gently toss cucumbers and strawberries in mixture. Arrange a portion over each lettuce leaf. Serves 4.

Note: If you don't have balsamic vinegar, use red wine vinegar plus 1 tsp (5 mL) sugar.

Spinach Casserole

Ruth Vriend is a vegetable grower who frequents a number of markets. She shared this casserole, a favorite in her family.

1 cup	sour cream	250 mL
1 cup	Cheddar cheese, grated	250 mL
1 1/2 oz	pkg dry onion soup	45 g
4 cups	fresh spinach, steamed	1 L

Preheat oven to 350 F (180 C). Chop spinach and press to drain. Mix sour cream and onion soup, and add to spinach, folding in well. Put 1/2 spinach mixture into a 9 inch (2 L) ungreased casserole. Sprinkle with 1/2 Cheddar. Make a second layer with remaining spinach and top with remaining cheese. Heat in oven until bubbly, about 20 minutes.

Note: Frozen spinach may be used in place of fresh. Swiss chard or beet greens may also be substituted.

Potato Pancakes

Vi Bretin is an avid gardener and cook, and her table at the Old Strathcona Farmers' Market is always surrounded by foodies demanding her potatoes.

2 cups	raw potatoes, grated	500 mL
1/4 cup	milk	50 mL
1	egg, beaten	1
2 tsp	flour	10 mL
1 tsp	salt	5 mL
	pepper to taste	
1 tbsp	onion, grated	15 mL

Mix together potatoes and milk. Let stand 5 minutes. Drain. Combine egg, flour and seasonings. Add to potatoes. Drop batter by 1/4 cupfuls (50 mL) onto a well-greased hot griddle. Brown both sides. Serve with pot roast and vegetables. Serves 4.

Apple-Glazed Chicken

Flora Hinse shared 60 years of experience in this recipe.

3	whole chicken breasts	3
1/4 cup	flour	50 mL
2 tsp	salt	10 mL
1/2 tsp	paprika	2 mL
1/4 tsp	pepper	1 mL
1/4 cup	butter, melted	50 mL
1 cup	applesauce	250 mL
1/4 cup	honey	50 mL
1 tbsp	lemon or orange juice	15 mL
1/2 tsp	salt	2 mL
1/4 tsp	nutmeg	1 mL
1/8 tsp	pepper	1/2 mL

Preheat oven to 350 F (180 C). Cut chicken breasts in half. Combine flour, salt and pepper in a bag. Shake chicken pieces in the bag to coat evenly. Place in a greased baking dish, skin-side up. Pour butter over chicken. Bake, uncovered, 30 minutes. Combine remaining ingredients and spread over chicken. Continue cooking 40 minutes longer, or until chicken is tender and brown. Baste frequently. Serves 6.

Grilled Chicken Rolls with Mustard Mayo

There are sandwiches, and then there's this–a creation I make with chicken fresh from a market vendor.

2	whole chicken breasts	2
1 tbsp	coarse grain mustard	15 mL
1 tbsp	chives, chopped	15 mL
2 tbsp	good mayonnaise	30 mL
4	crusty rolls	4
4	romaine lettuce leaves	4
	salt and pepper to taste	

Preheat broiler or barbecue. Skin, bone and halve chicken breasts and flatten slightly.

Stir together mustard, chives and mayonnaise. Dip 1 side chicken breasts in mixture, coating thoroughly. Grill 4 inches (10 cm) from heat, 5 to 7 minutes, brushing once during grilling.

Turn, brush with mustard mayo and grill another 5 to 7 minutes, basting once. Let chicken stand 5 minutes for juices to set.

Meanwhile slice rolls and brush with plain mayonnaise. Lay romaine leaves on bottom half of roll, place grilled chicken on top, add salt and pepper and top of roll. Goes well with cold beer. Serves 4.

Pork Tenderloin with Mushrooms and Mead

Since the first pioneer set foot on the prairies, people have been making wines from native fruits, notably saskatoons and chokecherries.

One enterprising Alberta wine firm is now producing Wild Rose Mead. If you can't find it in your part of the world, use another mead or even hard cider.

2 lb	pork tenderloin medallions	1 kg
2 tbsp	seasoned flour	30 mL
3 tbsp	butter	45 mL
1	onion, chopped	1
1/2 lb	white mushrooms, sliced	250 g
1 cup	mead (or hard cider)	250 mL
1 tbsp	rosemary	15 mL
2 tbsp	lemon juice	30 mL
2 tbsp	fresh parsley, chopped	30 mL

Dredge medallions with flour seasoned with salt, pepper and a hint of paprika. Sauté in butter until browned. Add mushrooms and onion and sauté for a few minutes. Add mead and rosemary, stir, cover and cook 20 minutes. Remove lid and simmer a few more minutes. When ready to serve add lemon juice and sprinkle with parsley. Serves 8.

Sun-Dried Herb Tomatoes

The flavor of a sun-dried tomato is quite different from canned or fresh, being sweeter and more intense. For sun-drying, the best tomatoes are the meaty little Italian plums. Use extra virgin olive oil and be prepared to trundle them around the house from one sunny spot to another.

12	Italian plum tomatoes	12
1 tbsp	salt (approximately)	15 mL
1 cup	white vinegar (approximately)	250 mL
1 cup	good Italian olive oil (approximately)	250 mL
2	garlic cloves	2
2	sprigs fresh basil or rosemary	2

Cut tomatoes in half. Lay them cut-side up on trays and salt lightly. Put out in the sun and allow tomatoes to dehydrate slowly. (Cover with cheesecloth or plastic screening to protect from insects and take trays in at night if there is heavy dew.) When tomatoes are dry and shriveled, dip in white vinegar, shaking off excess. Place in sterilized 1/2 qt (1/2 L) jars with garlic and your choice of herb, and cover completely with olive oil. For a long shelf life, process jars in a boiling water bath for 15 minutes. Makes about 2 cups (500 mL).

Rosemary Mint Sauce

This rosemary mint sauce is wonderful sprinkled on grilled lamb, chicken or roast loin of pork.

1 cup	rosemary vinegar	250 mL
2 tbsp	red wine vinegar	30 mL
3 tbsp	honey	45 mL
2 tbsp	vegetable oil	30 mL
1 cup	washed mint leaves, finely chopped	250 mL

Put everything in a small jar, cover and shake. Spoon over grilled meat. Keeps well in the refrigerator for 1 week. Makes about 2 cups.

Green Tomato Chutney

A delicious chutney with cold beef or chicken.

8 lb	green tomatoes, chopped	4 L
2 cups	green pepper, chopped	500 mL
1 cup	onion, chopped	250 mL
1 1/2 cups	sugar	375 mL
1 1/4 cups	cider vinegar	300 mL
4 tsp	salt	20 mL
1 tbsp	dry mustard	15 mL
1 tbsp	mustard seed	15 mL
1 1/2 tsp	celery seed	7 mL
1 tsp	turmeric	5 mL

Combine all ingredients in a large, heavy-bottomed, non-aluminum saucepan. Place over medium heat and stir until sugar is dissolved. Increase heat and cook briskly 25 minutes, stirring often to prevent mixture from sticking. Ladle into 4 hot, sterilized 1/2 qt (1/2 L) jars, filling to within 1/2 inch (1 cm) of top. Cover with clean lids and process in boiling water bath 15 minutes. Cool, label and store.

Tomato-Lime Chutney

This is so good you'll wish it would go twice as far. Serve with any grilled meat.

1 tbsp	oil	15 mL
1	small dry chili pepper, crumbled	1
1/2 tsp	cumin seed	2 mL
1/4 tsp	nutmeg	1 mL
1/4 tsp	mustard seed	1 mL
1 inch	fresh green ginger, grated	2 cm
4	large tomatoes, sliced very thin	4
1	fresh lime, rind and juice	1
1/3 cup	raisins or currants	75 mL
1/2 cup	sugar	125 ml
	salt to taste	

Heat oil in a saucepan. Add crumbled chili pepper, cumin seed, nutmeg, mustard seed and ginger. When the seeds start to jump in the oil, add tomatoes.

Grate lime rind, squeeze juice, and cut skin in quarters. Add to other ingredients in the pan. Simmer 15 minutes, stirring as needed to keep from sticking. Stir in raisins and sugar. Continue to simmer, stirring frequently, until mixture thickens, about 30 minutes. Cool and transfer to jars. Store in the refrigerator. Makes about 2 cups (500 mL).

Peach 'n' Honey Chutney

Brilliant color, vibrant flavor. Serve as relish with poultry or meats.

3 1/2 cups	fresh peaches, peeled and diced	875 mL
3 cups	apples, peeled and diced	750 mL
28 oz	can whole, peeled tomatoes	875 g
1 cup	green pepper, diced	250 g
1/4 cup	onion, chopped	50 mL
1 tsp	salt	5 mL
1/2 tsp	each, ground ginger and dry mustard	2 mL
1/2 cup	red wine vinegar	125 mL
3/4 cup	honey	175 mL
	Tabasco sauce (optional)	

Combine all ingredients except honey and Tabasco in a large kettle. Bring mixture to full rolling boil. Reduce heat but continue to boil. Cook, stirring occasionally, 30 minutes. Slowly stir in honey. Lower heat and simmer 30 minutes longer, or until mixture thickens. (Add Tabasco to taste, if desired.) Ladle into hot jars, leaving head space. Adjust caps. Process 15 minutes in boiling water bath. Cool. Refrigerate chutney after opening. Makes about 2 qt (2 L).

Fresh Cucumber Salsa

Every great sandwich needs a cucumber. If you get tired of slice-and-serve, try a fresh salsa made with cucumbers, tomatoes and onions. It goes well with any barbecued meat and can be stirred into a mashed avocado or used as a tortilla chip dip.

2	large tomatoes, finely chopped	2
1	small English cucumber, finely diced	1
1	small jalapeño pepper, minced	1
1 tbsp	cilantro leaves, chopped	15 mL
	juice and grated rind of 1 lime	
1 or 2	garlic cloves, minced	1 or 2
1/2 tsp	salt	2 mL

Mix everything together in a glass jar. Cover and refrigerate up to 3 days. If you can't find cilantro in the market, use a good bash of freshly chopped parsley. The flavor will be different, but good. Makes about 3 cups (750 mL).

FAST TRACK MENU

Onion Squares
Sausage and Bok Choy
Bananas with Cream and Cashews

Onion Squares

The market gardener who gave me this recipe recommended it with steak. But it's just as good with sausage and bok choy. For dessert–Bananas with Cream and Cashews.

2	large yellow onions, sliced	2
3 tbsp	butter	45 mL
2 cups	flour, sifted	500 mL
2 tsp	baking powder	10 mL
1 tsp	salt	5 mL
1/4 cup	shortening	50 mL
1/4 cup	fresh parsley, chopped	50 mL
1 cup	milk	250 mL
1/2 cup	Cheddar cheese, grated	125 mL
1/2 cup	sour cream	125 mL

Preheat oven to 425 F (220 C). Sauté onions in butter until tender. Do not brown.

Sift flour, baking powder and salt together. Cut in shortening until mixture is a fine crumble. Add parsley and milk. Stir only until all flour is moistened.

Spoon into a well-buttered 9 inch (2 L) pan. Spread onions on top and slather with sour cream. Sprinkle with cheese.

Bake 20 minutes. Cut into squares and serve hot. Serves 6.

Sausage and Bok Choy

From Yong Soo Jung, whose customers adore his fresh-picked bok choy, comes this wonderful combination.

1 lb	coarse garlic sausage	500 g
1 cup	water	250 mL
1	large head bok choy	1
3 tbsp	peanut oil	45 mL
2	large onion, sliced	2
1/4 cup	beef broth	50 mL
1/4 cup	cider or malt vinegar	50 mL
1 tbsp	soya sauce	15 mL
2 tsp	cornstarch	10 mL
1/4 tsp	hot red pepper flakes	1 mL

Slice sausage. Place in a frypan with 1 cup (250 mL) water. Heat to simmer and cook, covered, 10 minutes. Uncover the frypan. Cook over medium-low heat until water has evaporated and sausage is crispy at the skin. Drain on a paper towel.

Cut bok choy stalks into 1/2 inch (1 cm) wide pieces.

Heat wok and add oil. Add oinions and fry, stirring occasionally, over medium heat until limp and golden, about 10 minutes.

Meanwhile, mix broth, vinegar, soya sauce, cornstarch and pepper flakes in a small bowl. When onions are done, add bok choy. Stir-fry over medium heat until bok choy is crisp-tender, about 5 minutes. Add sausage. Add some broth mixture to cornstarch to dissolve, then stir mixture into the pan. Cook, stirring until sauce thickens. Serve immediately. Serves 6.

Bananas with Cream and Cashews

4	bananas	4
1/2 cup	cream	125 mL
1/2 cup	salted cahews, chopped	125 mL
3 tbsp	brown sugar	45 mL

Slice bananas, distributing them among 6 sauce dishes or fruit nappies. Drizzle each dish with a little cream, using 1/2 cup (125 mL) in all. Sprinkle cashews over bananas.

Sprinkle each serving with about 3 tbsp (45 mL) brown sugar. Serves 6.

CHAPTER 9
September

Back to Our Roots

September Recipes

Canadian cuisine must surely be one of the great mysteries of international politics.

Somehow it has been bruited about the international set that Canada, a little-known land mass somewhere north of Chicago, is locked in a perpetual deep freeze, populated by roving herds of wild-eyed caribou and Inuit who chew whale blubber while mushing their faithful dogs across the frozen tundra.

To some extent, we've become victims of our own success. Consider an average diplomatic banquet: Canadian diplomats strive to serve all-Canadian meals to trusting visitors. At issue is our national identity, and woe betide the chef whose menu neglects a province or territory.

Inevitably, the meal begins with smoked salmon from the West Coast, goes on to consommé of reindeer from the Yukon, Arctic *char en papilott*e from the Northwest Territories. Then it's on to roast buffalo from Alberta, with highbush cranberries from Manitoba and fiddleheads from New Brunswick.

I have visions of a frustrated German-born chef pacing his Ottawa kitchen and fuming, "Oh Canada, my home and recent land, have I neglected any major piece of real estate?"

Indeed he has. What about Nova Scotia? (Drag out the lobster.) Newfoundland? (Bring on the codfish.) P.E.I.? (Good Lord, he's forgotten the spuds.) Hence the popularity of that ubiquitous catch-all, Maritime Chowder. A timbale of wild rice will appease Ontario, and he can end the thing with maple-sugar-something from *La Belle Province*. Whew! *Tout fini!*

Alas, poor chef, not quite. Now an army of waiters must wheel out flaming pots of something called Royal Canadian Coffee and declare that it represents Labrador.

Enough, already. This is not cuisine–it's politics.

I think about those Canadian banquets sometimes. Times like the evenings spent in a local Thai restaurant, warming body and soul with a sizzling stir-fry. Or when I'm making bruschetta and minestrone for my kids. Or during times of great stress when I hunker gratefully over my all-time favorite comfort food, Hot-and-Sour Soup.

On the prairies, where I grew up, cod cheeks and fiddleheads were pretty scarce, but we did eat our quota of local specialties–perogies and cabbage rolls, sauerkraut and German sausages–and when we drove a few miles north we ran smack into a bevy of good Norwegian and Icelandic cooks whose pastries were to die for.

When I roast a chicken, I often put on a pot of cabbage rolls, too. They're part of my prairie roots, like saskatoon pie and homemade ice cream. (As for that well-known prairie dish, roast buffalo, the first time I ever ate it was at Canada Night in Frankfurt, Germany.)

Canada's multicultural nature is nowhere more evident than at our tables, and with a little help from our friends–the French, the Italians, the Vietnamese, the Ukrainians and other nationalities who populate this polyglot nation–a distinctive Canadian cuisine may yet be allowed to emerge. Bring on the Quesadillas, the Oliebollen, the Thai fried noodles.

Shrimp Starters

Cookbook author, teacher and columnist Susan Toy provided me with this scrumptious shrimp recipe.

1/2 lb	large shrimps in shell	250 g
l tsp	dry sherry	5 mL
pinch	white pepper	pinch
2	eggs, beaten	2
l cup	cornstarch	250 mL
1	thin slice fresh ginger root	1
3 cups	peanut oil	750 mL

Shell shrimps, leaving tail intact. Split shrimps lengthwise, but don't break apart. Rinse and discard intestinal vein. Pat dry with paper towels.

Place shrimps in a bowl and sprinkle with sherry and white pepper. Toss to mix.

Beat eggs, then pour into a shallow dish. Measure cornstarch into another shallow dish.

Place wok over high heat. Pour in oil and heat until vapor rises. Drop in slice of fresh ginger root. Once ginger is lightly browned, oil is ready for frying.

Dip shrimp 1 at a time into beaten eggs, then coat evenly with corn starch. Repeat a second time, then place into hot oil. Fry both sides to a golden brown. Transfer to a paper towel-lined platter to absorb excess oil. (Don't crowd shrimps during frying. You may have to divide them into 3 frying groups.)

Serve hot on a preheated plate. Sprinkle with a little spiced salt or your favorite dip. Serves 4 to 6 as an appetizer.

Swiss Onion Soup

This gently delicious brew was shared by a reader who was raised in the Ticino district of Switzerland, near the Italian border, where good cooks use stale bread cubes as a thickener in their onion soup.

6	big onions, chopped	6
1/2 cup	butter	125 mL
4 cups	milk	1 L
2 cups	water	500 mL
1/2 lb	Swiss cheese, grated	250 g
6	slices stale bread, cubed	6
	salt and pepper to taste	
1/2 tsp	sweet paprika	2 mL
	chives or green onion tops for garnish	

Cook but don't brown onions in butter until soft. Stir in milk and water, and bring to a simmer. Add bread, salt, pepper and paprika. Simmer 20 minutes. Add cheese and simmer over the lowest possible heat 10 minutes more, stirring occasionally. (Do not boil.) Garnish with fresh chopped chives or green onion tops. Serve with dark rye bread, lavishly buttered. This soup goes well with a crisp Alsatian white wine or with beer. Serves 6.

The Best Guacamole

The lovely jagged leaves of cilantro are not everybody's favorite herb. Some think it's soapy, but I find it a clean, refreshing taste. I love cilantro in salsa and chicken soup, with barbecued lamb and especially in guacamole.

2	large ripe avocados, pitted and mashed	2
	juice and grated peel of 1 lime	
1	large tomato, chopped	1
1	green onion, chopped	1
1	clove garlic, mashed	1
1	fresh jalapeño pepper, seeded and chopped	1
1 tbsp	cilantro, chopped	15 mL
	salt to taste	

Mix all ingredients thoroughly and serve immediately with taco chips or warm pita bread. Serves 6.

Bruschetta

Italians coming to Canada are surprised (not to say shocked) when they encounter for the first time our beloved mushy butter-soaked garlic bread. Their own idea of the same thing is a crisp bread, either toasted or fried, and often served with a glass of wine before dinner. It takes many forms and many names, depending on the region and the cook. This Umbrian version is crisp and full-flavored.

8	slices of day-old Italian bread	8
4	garlic cloves	4
	salt and pepper to taste	
1/2 cup	extra virgin olive oil	125 mL

Toast bread under a broiler, turning once.

Rub cut cloves of garlic on both sides of toast while still hot. Discard garlic.

Sprinkle lightly with salt and pepper. Brush generously with warm extra virgin olive oil and serve at once as an appetizer with your favorite tipple. Serves 8.

Fried Wine Bread

Yet another variation on the Italian bread theme is this Sicilian fried bread that works well as a simple appetizer with amarone, valpolicella or bardolino wine. Do not be tempted to fry it in olive oil, as the flavor will be too heavy.

1	loaf day-old Italian bread	1
1/2 cup	dry red wine	125 mL
1 cup	peanut or canola oil	250 mL
	coarse salt to taste	

Sprinkle both sides of bread with wine. (Do not soak.)

Add oil to a heavy frypan over high heat. Fry bread just until it forms a golden crust, but does not burn. Turn bread over and fry until second side is also golden brown.

As bread browns, remove onto layers of paper towels to absorb excess oil and sprinkle with coarse salt. Cut bread slices in half and serve immediately as an appetizer or with any hearty soup. It also goes well with a plate of fried peppers and sausages. Serves 8.

Four Crostini

Crostini, which means crusts, is a toasted bread appetizer from Italy, topped with delicious spreads. Here are 4 of the simplest and the best. Be generous with the bread–cut slices 1 inch (2 cm) thick.

CROSTINI WITH THREE CHEESES

1 cup	Ricotta cheese	250 mL
1/2 cup	Parmesan cheese	125 mL
1/2 cup	Gorgonzola cheese	125 mL
1/2 tsp	oregano	2 mL
1 tbsp	extra virgin olive oil	15 mL
1	clove garlic, minced	1
6	slices Italian bread, toasted	6

Mix cheeses then add other ingredients. Put in a blender and blend until smooth. Spread on crostini and grill until bubbly. Serves 6.

CROSTINI WITH DICED SWEET PEPPERS

1	sweet red pepper	1
1	sweet green pepper	1
1 tbsp	olive oil	15
1	clove garlic, crushed	1
5 or 6	ripe olives, chopped	5 or 6
	dried basil to taste	
6	slices Italian bread, toasted	6

Dice both peppers, then sauté quickly in oil with garlic and olives. Sprinkle with basil. Spread on crostini and grill to reheat. Serves 6.

CROSTINI WITH PLUM TOMATOES AND BASIL

2 cups	plum tomatoes	500 mL
2 tbsp	extra virgin olive oil	30 mL
1	clove garlic, mashed	1
1 tsp	salt	5 mL
1/2 cup	fresh basil or parsley, chopped	125 mL
6	slices Italian bread, toasted	6

Peel and finely dice tomatoes, then toss with oil. Mash garlic clove into salt and basil or parsley. Spread on crostini. Serve hot or cold. Serves 6.

RIPE OLIVE CROSTINI

2 cups	pitted black olives, roughly chopped	500 mL
1 tbsp	extra virgin olive oil	15 mL
1	clove garlic	1
2	anchovy filets, roughly chopped	2
	pepper to taste	
1 tbsp	capers, chopped	15 mL
6	slices Italian bread, toasted	6

Purée all ingredients in a blender. Pile generously on crostini and serve at room temperature. Serves 6.

Quesadillas with Tomato Salsa

Kids love these things, even with the hot sauce. If you're short of time, use a prepared salsa.

QUESADILLAS

4	flour tortillas	4
4 tbsp	butter	60 mL
1 cup	cheese (Jack or Cheddar), grated	250 mL

Melt butter in a wide, round skillet over medium heat. Put 1 tortilla in the skillet and sprinkle cheese onto half. Fold tortilla over, press flat and move to one side of the pan. Place another tortilla in the skillet (it doesn't have to lie flat) and repeat the process. Brown both sides. Place quesadillas in warm oven until served.

SALSA

2	medium tomatoes, chopped	2
2	scallions, sliced	2
1/2 cup	green chilies, diced	125 mL
1/4 cup	fresh cilantro leaves	50 mL
1	avocado, sliced	1
1/2 cup	sour cream	125 mL

Toss together tomatoes, scallions, chilies and cilantro. Place avocado slices on hot quesadillas. Spoon on sour cream. Spoon salsa over and serve. Serves 4.

Las Brizas Salad in Tortilla Bowls

There are many versions of this salad floating about in Mexican restaurants. Most of them are pretty good, but this one has become a favorite among my readers.

SALAD

6 cups	iceberg lettuce, torn	1.5 L
1	tomato, chopped	1
1 cup	Cheddar cheese, grated	250 mL
1/2 cup	pitted ripe olives, sliced	125 mL
2	avocados, seeded and peeled	2
1/2 cup	whipped salad dressing	125 mL
2	slices crisp bacon, crumbled	2
2 tbsp	canned green chilies, chopped	30 mL
1 tbsp	lemon juice	15 mL
1	clove garlic, minced	1
1 lb	ground beef, cooked and drained	500 g
1	onion, chopped	1
2 cups	canned kidney beans, drained	500 mL
8 oz	bottle hot taco sauce	250 mL
4	tortilla bowls	4

Toss lettuce, tomato, 3/4 cup (175 mL) cheese and olives in a large bowl. Cover and chill.

Mash avocados. Stir in salad dressing, bacon, green chili peppers, lemon juice and garlic. (If necessary, stir in 1 to 2 tbsp (15 to 30 mL) milk to make dressing desired consistency.) Cover and chill.

Mix together cooked ground beef, onion, beans and taco sauce. Cover and simmer 10 minutes, stirring occasionally. Cool slightly.

Place lettuce mixture in tortilla bowls. Spoon warm meat mixture on top, then spoon dressing on top of meat. Sprinkle with remaining cheese. Makes 4 servings.

TORTILLA BOWLS

Cut 8 circles of foil, 10 inches (25 cm) in diameter. In a large skillet heat 4 tortillas of the same size as foil, 1 at a time, over low heat 1 minute, or until just pliable. Place each tortilla on 2 foil circles. Bring foil up in the shape of ruffled bowls. Place bowls on an ungreased baking sheet. Bake in a 350 F (180 C) oven about 10 minutes, or until crisp. Transfer bowls to a wire rack to cool. Remove foil. Makes 4.

Thai Noodle Salad

From a generous Thai cook, here's a noodle salad that will banish all those wishy-washy pasta salads from your memory.

1 lb	thin noodles	500 g
1/4 cup	sesame seed oil	50 mL
2 tbsp	tahini (sesame seed paste)	30 mL
1/2 cup	teryaki sauce	125 mL
4	green onions, finely chopped	4
4	cloves garlic, crushed	4
1 tbsp	ginger, grated	15 mL

Cook noodles only until *al dente*. Rinse well in cold water.

Heat oil and toss noodles in it until thoroughly coated. Add tahini and toss well. Remove from pan and let cool.

Combine other ingredients and toss well with noodles. Serve cold. Serves 4.

Moroccan Orange Salad

Orange flower water is an essence of orange blossoms, one of life's little luxuries. Traditionally, it comes in a glass bottle in an exquisite shade of blue and is available in specialty food sections. A few drops on a sliced orange is a taste of old Morocco.

6	seedless oranges	6
	juice of 1 lemon	
1 tsp	lemon peel, finely grated	5 mL
dash	cinnamon	dash
1/4 cup	liquid honey	50 mL
2 tsp	orange flower water	10 mL
	fresh mint (optional)	

Peel oranges, completely removing all membrane. Slice over a bowl so none of the juice is lost.

Add lemon juice, peel, cinnamon, honey and orange water. Cover dish and let fruit macerate 1 hour.

To serve, arrange orange slices on 4 chilled plates. Garnish with a leaf of fresh mint. Serves 4.

Mast Va Hkiar

This simple Iranian salad is traditionally served ice cold. It's excellent with barbecued lamb or chicken and a basket of warm pita bread.

1	large English cucumber, shredded	1
1/4 cup	red bell pepper, minced	50 mL
2	green onions, including tops, minced	2
1 tbsp	fresh dill, minced	15 mL
1 tbsp	fresh cilantro, minced	15 mL
1 tsp	sugar	5 mL
1 tbsp	fresh lime juice	15 mL
1 cup	plain yogurt	250 mL
	dill or cilantro sprigs for garnish (optional)	

Mix all ingredients except garnish together and put into the freezer. Stir every 10 minutes for 45 minutes to 1 hour. (It will begin to form the odd ice crystal). Mound onto a serving dish and garnish with sprigs of dill or cilantro. Serve immediately. Serves 6 to 8.

Rice with Chilies and Cheese

Fast and easy. Serve with raw vegetables and your favorite dip.

2 1/2 cups	cooked rice	625 mL
	salt and pepper to taste	
dash	oregano	dash
1/2 cup	diced green chilies	125 mL
1	green onion, chopped	1
2 cups	sour cream	500 mL
1 cup	Cheddar cheese, grated	250 mL
	paprika and fresh parsley for garnish	

Preheat oven to 350 F (180 C). Mix salt, pepper and oregano with rice. Stir green chilies and onions with sour cream and cheese. Fold into rice. Bake 30 minutes, uncovered, in a buttered casserole or mold. (You may wish to put a bit more cheese on top during the last 5 minutes.) Garnish with parsley and paprika. Serves 4 to 6.

Aruba Chicken

This scrumptious Caribbean chicken stew came to me from food lover Brenda Haley.

1	broiler chicken, cut up	1
1	Spanish onion, chopped	1
2 tbsp	oil	30 mL
1 lb	ham, cubed	500 g
2 tbsp	red wine	30 mL
2 cups	water	500 mL
1 cup	tomato sauce	250 mL
1/4 cup	coconut	50 mL
1 tsp	salt	5 mL
1/2 tsp	red pepper, crushed	2 mL
4	whole cloves	4
1	bay leaf	1
2 lb	sweet potatoes	1 kg
1/4 tsp	thyme	1 mL
2	bananas, peeled and sliced	2
	coconut curls, toasted (optional)	

Sauté onion in oil until golden. Remove and reserve.

Brown chicken pieces. Add reserved onion, ham and wine. Stir in water, tomato sauce, coconut and salt. Tie red pepper, cloves and bay leaf in a cheesecloth. Add to stew. Bring to boil and immediately lower heat. Cover and simmer 15 minutes.

Meanwhile, peel sweet potatoes and cut into 1/2 inch (1 cm) slices. Add to stew, pushing them down into liquid. Simmer about 30 minutes longer, until meat and potatoes are tender. Add thyme and bananas.

Simmer 5 to 10 minutes longer. Remove spice bag. Arrange stew in a serving dish. Garnish with toasted coconut curls. Serves 6.

Tori No Sanmi Yaki
(THREE FLAVORED JAPANESE CHICKEN)

Gayle Seagrave was an *Edmonton Journal* Recipe Contest winner with this beautiful Japanese chicken dish.

3 tbsp	sesame seeds	45 mL
2	cloves garlic, crushed	2
1/2	small dry chili pepper, seeds removed	1/2
1/4 tsp	fresh ginger root, grated	1 mL
1/4 cup	dry sherry or saki	50 mL
1/3 cup	soya sauce	75 mL
1/4 cup	honey	50 mL
2	boneless whole chicken breasts	2
1	green pepper, cut in strips	1
1 tbsp	vegetable oil	15 mL
12	thin lemon slices	12
	green pepper for garnish	
2 cups	steamed rice	500 mL

Preheat oven to 325 F (160 C). Toast sesame seeds until amber. Mash seeds with garlic, chili pepper and ginger until a paste forms.

Split chicken breasts into 2 pieces, leaving skin on. Place breasts in a non-metal shallow pan and marinate in sauce, covered, 4 hours in the refrigerator, turning occasionally.

Remove to a greased 9 x 9 inch (22 x 22 cm) baking dish. Bake 25 minutes, basting occasionally with marinade. Broil 5 minutes until glazed.

Meanwhile sauté green pepper strips in vegetable oil just until slightly wilted. Slice each breast piece diagonally into 4 pieces. Arrange on a heated platter. Tuck lemon slices between chicken pieces. Garnish with green pepper. Serve with steamed rice. Serves 4.

Oliebollen

Paul DeGroot has his roots in Holland.

"The Dutch have an ironic twist of mind, which is perhaps why they call one of their favorite foods 'grease balls'. In the original language it's 'oliebollen' (OH-LEE-BOW-LEN). They're basically apple fritters, with the emphasis on fritter, since they often don't include apples," Paul tells me.

4 cups	flour	1 L
1 1/2	cakes of yeast	1.5
2	eggs	2
3/4 tbsp	salt	12 mL
2 cups	milk, warmed	500 mL
1/2 lb	currants	250 g
1/2 lb	raisins	250 g
1	apple, diced	1

Sift flour and salt in a big bowl. Dissolve yeast in warm water. Make a hole in middle of flour and break eggs into hole. Add yeast and start stirring with a wooden spoon. Slowly add warm milk. Keep stirring until all milk and flour are mixed and dough is smooth. Stir some more. Add currants, raisins and diced apple. Cover and let rise in a warm place 1 to 2 hours.

Heat deep frying oil to 350 F (180 C). Drop 1 inch (2 cm) balls of dough in hot oil and cook for approximately 7 minutes, until golden brown and done. Drain. Serve warm with powdered sugar. Serves 6.

FAST TRACK MENU

Grilled Tomatoes
Grilled Cheese Sandwich with Onion
Baked Apple Pudding

Grilled Tomatoes

2	tomatoes, halved	2
2 tsp	butter	10 mL
	basil, salt and pepper to taste	

Preheat broiler. Dot tomato halves with butter. Sprinkle with basil, salt and pepper. Broil 4 inches (10 cm) from heat until bubbly. Serves 4.

Grilled Cheese Sandwich with Onion

Once, for a big party, I made dozens of tiny mozzarella sandwiches, fried them in butter, and served them screamin' hot with cold chardonnay. It was a fabulous combination. But for times of stress, a bigger, bolder sandwich like this is needed.

1 tbsp	Dijon mustard	15 mL
1 tbsp	mayonnaise	15 mL
8	slices wholewheat bread	8
2 cups	Cheddar cheese, grated	500 mL
2 cups	mozzarella, grated	500 mL
8	slices Spanish onion	8
2 to 3 tbsp	soft butter	30 to 45 mL

Mix mustard and mayonnaise and spread on bread.

Sprinkle cheese evenly over 4 slices. Top with onion and remaining slices, mustard-mayo side down. Spread outside of bread with soft butter.

Brown sandwiches on both sides until cheese melts. Serve with dill pickles. Serves 4.

Baked Apple Pudding

2	large apples, peeled and chopped	2
1 cup	flour	250 mL
1/2 cup	sugar	125 mL
2 tsp	baking powder	10 mL
pinch	salt	pinch
1/2 cup	nuts (almonds or walnuts), chopped	125 mL
1/2 cup	milk	125 mL
2 tbsp	butter, melted	30 mL
1 tsp	vanilla	5 ml
1/2 cup	brown sugar, packed	125 mL
1 1/2 cups	boiling water	375 mL
1 tbsp	butter	15 mL

Combine flour, sugar, baking powder and salt in a bowl. Stir in apples and nuts. Stir in milk, melted butter and vanilla. Mix together thoroughly. Spoon batter into a greased 9 x 9 inch (22 x 22 cm) pan. Combine sugar, boiling water and additional butter. Stir until sugar is dissolved and butter is melted. Pour carefully over unbaked batter. Bake at 350 F (180 C) 40 minutes. Serve warm. Serves 4 generously.

CHAPTER 10
October

Food, Glorious Food

October Recipes

"Food, glorious food, hot sausage and mustard..." Oliver Twist had the right idea. That's exactly how food should be–simple, welcoming and gloriously, splendidly comforting.

Writing about food involves the remembrance of things past, evoked by the subtlest taste, the frailest whiff. The smell of minerals and chocolate in a certain bottle of bordeaux takes me back to the Rexall Drustore in Quill Lake, Saskatchewan, *circa* 1960, where prescriptions were filled among the boxes of Black Magic Chocolates.

Nostalgia is one of the by-products of good food, and at this time of year, when the frost is on the pumpkin, I can't help feeling a twinge of nostalgia for Mrs. Odelein's cow.

There's little doubt that she was a contented animal, grazing away in the back pasture with nothing more to worry about than which clover to chomp next.

Fame came to Mrs. Odelein's cow because of her cream, which was so sweet and thick that getting on the preferred customer list was trickier than being on a good chicken and egg list. It was right up there with beating out Vera Poulton's potatoes at the horticultural show, which (as anyone who ever ate a Poulton potato could tell you) was impossible.

The cream arrived on Saturday. That was the day Mrs. Odelein came into town to shop in the heady environs of Main Street, where both the Co-Op and the Red and White kept their doors open until 9 pm. Saturday was also the day the town band held concerts in the parking lot beside Anne's Coffee Shop, always leading off with *Colonel Bogie*.

Considering the giddy social pace of Main Street on Saturday night, we seldom got into the cream jar until Sunday.

By Sunday, it was thicker.

At 50 cents for an Imperial quart, that jar of cream was probably the bargain of the century. It did not pour; it had to be scooped like soft cream cheese. And while it waited there in the spoon, momentarily poised over a slice of pumpkin pie, it had the color and sheen of ivory.

The way to eat it was plain, on berries as they came into season, on pies and in certain casseroles involving potatoes and a lot of cheese. Whipping it was trickier than getting on the list in the first place because it was already so thick and would turn to butter in the blink of an eye.

I have never had cream like it since. Given the way we eat now, I'm not sure what I'd do with it if I did have some. Probably gentle creatures like Mrs. Odelein's cow have all been put on diets. But I can still taste it, in October, when I get my first whiff of oven-fresh pumpkin pie.

Apricot Mustard with Garlic

A Chinese chef who spent years in Southeast Asia gave me this zingy Oriental mustard. It gives a whole new meaning to barbecued duck, pork or grilled sausage.

2 cups	dry mustard	500 mL
1/3 cup	flour	75 mL
2 cups	apricot jam	500 mL
1 cup	dried apricots, diced	250 mL
3/4 cup	dry sherry	175 mL
1/3 cup	soya sauce	75 mL
4	garlic cloves, minced	4
1 tsp	Tabasco sauce	5 mL
3/4 tsp	ground ginger	3 mL

In a double boiler, blend mustard and flour. Add remaining ingredients and mix well. Cook over simmering water until thickened, about 10 minutes, stirring often. Pour into glass containers and cover tightly. Store in a cold dark place. Makes about 6 cups (1.5 L).

Hot Sausage Balls

An easy snack with drinks, these spicy little sausage balls are like money in the bank for a busy host.

1 lb	hot bulk sausage	500 g
3 cups	buttermilk biscuit baking mix	750 mL
1 1/2 cups	sharp Cheddar cheese, grated	375 mL

Mix together ingredients and roll into 1 inch (2 cm) balls, place on cookie sheet and freeze until firm. Store in plastic bags in freezer.

To serve, bake frozen balls at 350 F (180 C) about 15 minutes, or until lightly browned. Serve with hot mustard. Makes 5 to 6 dozen sausage balls.

Pumpkin Soup

Here's a fast version of this classic fall dish.

2 cups	cooked pumpkin purée	500 mL
2 tbsp	tomato paste	30 mL
10 oz	can cream of celery soup	284 mL
2 cups	whole milk	30 mL
1 tsp	curry powder	5 mL
1/2 tsp	nutmeg, freshly grated	2 mL
	salt and pepper to taste	
	croutons and parsley for garnish	
1	pumpkin (optional)	1

Whisk together in a saucepan all ingredients except croutons and parsley, and heat to simmer, whisking constantly to keep pumpkin from scorching. Correct seasoning with salt and pepper.

Serve in small bowls garnished with croutons and parsley. Serves 6.

For a special harvest touch, serve in a pumpkin. Wash a medium-sized hollowed pumpkin and rub skin with vegetable oil. Pour boiling water into pumpkin to half fill it. Place pumpkin in a 300 F (150 C) oven about 10 minutes. Drain and put on a tray surrounded by fall leaves and red berries (mountain ash works well). Pour in soup. When serving, scoop a bit of pumpkin flesh into each bowl.

Wild Rice with Duck Salad

This salad always reminds me of fall days on the prairies when we'd spend Sunday evening driving the back roads spotting ducks so my dad would know where to go hunting early the next morning.

1/3 cup	wild rice	75 mL
1 1/2 cups	water	375 mL
1/3 cup	long grain rice	75 mL
1 1/2 cups	cooked duck breast, sliced	375 mL
2	oranges, peeled and sectioned	2
1	stalk celery, sliced	1
1/2 cup	fresh parsley, minced	125 mL
1/4 cup	green onions, sliced	50 mL
1/4 cup	walnut oil or salad oil	50 mL
3 tbsp	frozen orange juice concentrate, thawed	45 mL
1 tbsp	cider vinegar	15 mL
1 tbsp	Dijon mustard	15 mL
1/4 tsp	each, salt and cracked pepper	1 mL
l/2 cup	walnuts, broken	125 mL
	red leaf lettuce	
4	orange twists for garnish	4

Run cold water over uncooked wild rice in a strainer, lifting rice to rinse well. In a medium saucepan combine wild rice and water. Bring to boil, then reduce heat. Cover and simmer 20 minutes. Stir in long grain rice. Return to boiling, then reduce heat. Cover and simmer about 20 minutes more, or until rice is tender. Cool slightly.

In a large mixing bowl combine warm rice, duck, orange sections, celery, parsley and onion.

For dressing combine oil, orange juice, vinegar, mustard, salt and pepper in a screw-top jar. Shake well. Pour dressing over rice mixture and toss lightly. Cover and chill 4 hours or overnight.

To serve, mix in walnuts. Line 4 salad plates with lettuce leaves. Spoon rice mixture onto the plates. Garnish with orange twists. Serves 4.

Note: Turkey may be used in place of duck. Chinese barbecued duck is also delicious in this salad.

Onion Tart with Three Cheeses

For the last picnic of the year, this onion tart is as good cold as it is hot. Use a frozen pie shell to save time.

9 inch	pie shell	22 cm
2 tbsp	butter	30 mL
3	large onions, thinly sliced	3
3	large eggs	3
1 1/2 cups	milk	375 mL
1/4 tsp	nutmeg, freshly grated	1 mL
	salt and pepper to taste	
1/4 lb	Cheddar cheese, diced	125 g
1/2 lb	Gruyère cheese, diced	250 g
1/2 cup	Parmesan cheese, freshly grated	125 mL

Preheat oven to 350 degrees F (175 C). Melt butter in a large frypan. Add onions and cook until soft. (Do not brown.) Drain on paper towels to eliminate excess moisture.

Beat eggs, milk and nutmeg together. Season with salt and pepper.

Arrange onions in pie shell. Pour egg mixture over onions and sprinkle with Cheddar and Gruyère. Dust top with Parmesan.

Bake 35 to 45 minutes until filling is set and top is golden. Let cool slightly before cutting. Serves 8.

Note: This recipe is even better with puff pastry. Roll 1/8 inch (3 mm) thick, coat pie pan with 1 tbsp (15 mL) butter, then fit pastry into it. Trim excess and chill crust at least 30 minutes before filling. Continue as above.

Spiced Fruit Compote

For brunch or an easy dessert, here's a favorite. The raisins plump up until they're like very juicy grapes. If you wish to reduce the calories, use sugar-free ginger ale.

1	lemon, sliced	1
1/2 cup	pitted prunes	125 mL
1 cup	dried apricots	250 mL
1/2 cup	dried apples	125 mL
1 cup	golden raisins	250 mL
1/2 cup	sugar	125 mL
4 cups	ginger ale	1 L
1 tsp	allspice	5 mL
6	whole cloves	6
1	cinnamon stick, broken into 3 pieces	1
1	fresh ginger, thinly sliced	1

Put fruits, sugar, ginger ale and spices in a medium saucepan.

If necessary, add a little cold water. (The fruit should be covered with liquid.) Bring to boil, then reduce heat and simmer, covered, until fruit has absorbed most of the juice and is plump and tender. (Time will vary, depending upon how dry fruit is.) Add more water if necessary, keeping fruit covered at all times.

Before serving adjust sweetness to taste.

Serve with softly whipped cream or *creme fraiche*. Serves 8.

Baked Onions

There was a time when I would have turned up my nose at any recipe using canned soup. But reality has set in and life is easier now. Try these baked onions and you'll see why.

4	large onions	4
1/2 cup	condensed cream of chicken soup, undiluted	125 mL
1/4 cup	honey	50 mL
1/2 cup	water	125 mL
1 tsp	salt	5 mL
1/4 tsp	pepper	1 mL
1/4 tsp	ground ginger	1 mL

Peel and cut onions in half. Combine soup, honey, water, salt, pepper and ginger, and pour over onions. Cover and bake in a 350 F (180 C) oven 1 hour, or until tender. Baste twice while cooking. Serve with any roast or grilled meat. Serves 8.

Squash Gratin

Squash is so beautiful to look at that it's almost a shame to cook it, but this is so good I never mind the sacrifice.

2 1b	hubbard squash, cooked and puréed	1 kg
1/4 cup	butter, melted	50 mL
1	small onion, minced	1
1/2	green bell pepper, minced	0.5
1/2 cup	whipped salad dressing	125 mL
1/2 cup	Cheddar cheese, grated	125 mL
	salt and pepper to taste	

Whip together all ingredients. Pile into a buttered baking dish and bake at 325 F (160 C) 30 minutes. Serves 6.

Note: This may be done with 3 acorn squash, steaming squash until tender, then scooping out flesh and reserving shells. Continue as above and pile back into shells.

Barbecued Sausage Kabobs with Yellow Peppers and Plums

Sometimes the best barbecues are in the fall when the days have a definite nip and you can enjoy the louder, gutsier flavors of the season.

1	ring coarse garlic sausage	1
1	yellow bell pepper	1
4	blue plums	4
l/4 cup	fruit chutney	50 mL
1 tsp	Dijon mustard	5 mL
2 tsp	chili sauce	10 mL
4 drops	Tabasco sauce	4 drops

Cut sausage into small cross-wise pieces. Cut pepper into small squares. Halve and seed plums. Thread sausage, peppers and plums on 4 metal skewers.

Chop any chutney fruit into small bits. In a small pan, combine chutney, mustard, chili sauce and Tabasco. Heat, stirring until melted. Brush mixture over kabobs and grill about 4 inches (10 cm) from heat until sausages begin to sputter and brown. Brush with additional sauce, turn and cook other side 2 to 3 minutes. Serve hot with Italian bread or Kaiser rolls. Serves 4.

Chicken Breasts in Maple Syrup

Maple syrup gives this chicken dish a rich golden glaze, perfect for an autumn dinner. Supercook David McGill adapted it from an old Canadian recipe first published in the *Laura Secord Cookbook*.

4	chicken breasts	4
1/2 cup	flour, seasoned with salt and pepper	125 mL
3	large mushrooms, finely chopped	3
1/2 cup	ham, finely diced	125 mL
1	green onion, minced	1
1/3 cup	butter	75 mL
1 cup	onion, thinly sliced	250 mL
pinch	savory	pinch
4 tbsp	maple syrup	60 mL
1/2 cup	water	125 mL

Preheat oven to 350 F (180 C). Bone chicken breasts and roll in seasoned flour. Set aside.

Fry mushrooms, ham and green onion in 1 1/2 tbsp (25 mL) butter 2 to 3 minutes, or until mushrooms are tender.

Slit thick portion of each chicken breast and insert one spoonful of ham mixture. Pinch edges together to seal. Brown in a frypan in 1/4 cup (50 mL) butter. Remove chicken and add onion to the pan. Fry until slightly browned.

Arrange chicken breasts in a small casserole dish. Top with onion, sprinkle with savory and spoon 1 tbsp (15 mL) maple syrup over each breast.

Deglaze the frypan with water. Pour over chicken. Bake, uncovered, in a 350 F (180 C) oven for 30 minutes. Serves 4.

Pork Chops with Rhubarb Dressing

For me, this dish has all the aroma and flavor of autumn, so I make it with frozen rhubarb when the nights start to get chilly.

1/2 tsp	dried rosemary, crushed	2 mL
	salt and pepper to taste	
2 tbsp	oil	30 mL
6	boneless pork loin chops, 1 inch (2 cm) thick	6
4	slices bread, diced	4
3/4 cup	brown sugar, firmly packed	175 mL
1/2 tsp	cinnamon	2 mL
1/4 tsp	allspice	1 mL
2 cups	rhubarb, diced	500 mL
1	onion, diced	1
3 tbsp	flour	45 mL

Mix together rosemary, salt and pepper. Sprinkle evenly over chops.

Heat oil in a frypan over medium-high heat. Add chops and brown both sides. Set aside with drippings.

Stir together bread cubes, brown sugar, cinnamon, allspice, rhubarb, onion and flour. Spread 1/2 mixture in a greased 9 x 13 inch (3 L) baking dish. Arrange chops on top. Spoon over 3 tbsp (45 mL) of drippings (adding water if necessary to make this amount). Top with remaining mixture. Cover and bake in a 350 F (180 C) oven 45 minutes. Uncover and bake 15 minutes longer. Serves 6.

Lazy Lemon Squares

When the days grow shorter, there's nothing like a pot of tea and a lemon square about 4 o'clock. This recipe originated with the Lazy Gourmet in Vancouver and rapidly moved east.

CRUST

1 cup	butter		250 mL
1/3 cup	sugar		75 mL
1 3/4 cups	flour		425 mL
l/2 cup	almonds, crushed		125 mL

FILLING

4	eggs	4
1/3 cup	lemon juice	75 mL
1 tsp	lemon peel, finely grated	5 mL
1 1/4 cups	sugar	300 mL
1/3 cup	flour	75 mL
1 tsp	baking powder	5 mL

Combine ingredients for crust until crumbly and press into bottom of a 9 x 13 inch (3 L) pan. Bake for 20 minutes at 350 F (180 C) until light brown.

Mix eggs, lemon juice and sugar. Sift flour and baking powder together, add to filling and mix well. Spread mixture over crust and bake at 350 F (180 C) 25 minutes. Cool before cutting into squares. Be careful not to overbake. Serves about 10.

Brandied Peaches

Use the last freestone peaches of the year and the best French brandy for these sweet and spicy peaches. They make a great gift for ice cream lovers.

2 cups	sugar	500 mL
2 cups	water	500 mL
1 cup	lemon juice	250 mL
2 tbsp	whole cloves	30 mL
3	cinnamon sticks, broken	3
1 tsp	allspice	5 mL
1/2 cup	brandy	125 mL
2 qt	fresh peaches	2 L

Combine sugar, water, lemon juice and spices. Bring to boil, reduce heat, and simmer about 10 minutes. Cut peaches in half and remove pits. Pack into l qt (1 L) canning jars. Add brandy to hot syrup. Pour syrup over peaches, leaving spices in. Refrigerate 1 day to blend flavors. Serve over ice cream. Makes 2 qts (2 L).

Chianti Pears

Lilliana is a great Tuscan cook who lives just south of Florence, Italy, in the Chianti district. Her pears are famous in neighboring villages. Naturally, she uses a chianti classico for these, but you can substitute any good dry red wine.

6	pears , peeled	6
1 cup	water	250 mL
1 cup	red wine	250 mL
1/4 cup	sugar	50 mL
	juice of 1/2 lemon	
2	sticks cinnamon	2
2	whole cloves	2
	mint sprigs (optional)	

In a large saucepan, combine ingredients, except pears and mint.
Bring to boil. Add pears, reduce heat and simmer until tender. Let cool.
Serve in glass dessert dishes garnished with sprigs of mint. Serves 6.

FAST TRACK MENU

Popovers with Fresh Herbs

Serve these hot. They're a meal in themselves.

POPOVERS

3 tbsp	butter, melted	45 mL
3	eggs	3
1 1/2 cups	milk	375 mL
1 1/2 cups	flour, sifted	375 mL
3/4 tsp	salt	4 mL
4 drops	Tabasco sauce	4 drops
1 tbsp	fresh chives, chopped	15 mL
1 tbsp	fresh parsley, chopped	15 mL
2/3 cup	Parmesan cheese, freshly grated	150 mL

Preheat oven to 450 F (230 C). Use 1/2 butter to grease 8 muffin cups. In a mixing bowl whisk together eggs, milk and remaining melted butter.

Gradually add flour, whisking until smooth. Whisk in salt, Tabasco, chives, parsley and all but 2 tbsp (30 mL) of Parmesan.

Place the buttered muffin tin in the preheated oven until very hot and butter is sizzling but not browned, about 3 minutes. Pour about 1/4 cup (50 mL) of batter into each cup. Sprinkle batter with reserved Parmesan. Bake 15 minutes, then lower heat to 350 F (180 C) and continue baking until puffed and golden brown, about 15 minutes longer. Makes 8 popovers. Serves 4.

FILLING

10 oz	pkg cauliflower in cheese sauce, frozen	300 g
2 cups	ham, diced	500 mL

Cook cauliflower according to package directions. Fold in diced ham and heat.

Slit popovers and fill.

CHAPTER 11
November

The Staff of Life

November Recipes

On November mornings in Paris, the windows of 8 rue de Cherche-Midi are covered with steam, but you can still see the fat round loaves of bread in the window.

These loaves, with their whorls and squiggles and bunches of grapes sculptured in dough on the top, are so beautiful that even people with no intention of buying will stop to admire.

In a small cellar beneath the shop, a young baker has been tending the wood-fired ovens since 3 am, and the smell of fresh bread comes curling up the narrow staircase into the shop, which is also small and hot, and always crowded. Already, a long line of customers winds from the sidewalk through the door all the way to the cashier. They're grateful to be out of the windy street and into a place that feels so warm and smells so good.

This is the home turf of Lional Poilane, the busiest baker in Paris. Going into his cellar is rather like descending into hell—stone walls, a haze of heat, a nearly-naked baker stoking the ovens. His body is gray-white with the fine dusting of flour that covers him from head to foot, giving him a ghostly look, and he's lean from working in the intense heat, shoveling the big loaves in and out, in and out, his right arm working like a well-oiled machine.

Other loaves wait, rising in big bowls with reed baskets upended on top and the strong, living dough pushing hard against them, lifting the baskets higher and higher.

Lional Poilane's bread, like all bread, has personality. It has the baker's signature all over it. The bread I bake is different from my mother's and my grandmother's before her, and none of them were like anybody else's.

Grandma used potato water, Mom didn't. I liked Mom's best, for no good reason except that she baked on Saturday, and when I came in from the weekly trauma of my piano lesson and smelled it baking, I knew life was not so bad after all.

Good bread is the ultimate comforter and sustainer. There's nothing like the potent incense of rising dough and freshly baked loaves. There's nothing like it for making a hungry stomach feel coddled and cherished. Every child should be taught bread-making as one of the essential life skills, along with reading, writing, and cooking an egg.

Food Processor Bread

Making your own bread is a creative and therapeutic activity. Here's a loaf I like to make whenever I have time or there's need for a small benchmark in my week. It's good with soup or jam, wonderful with stew and excellent for mopping up gravy if you do that sort of thing.

1 tbsp	molasses	15 mL
1/4 cup	lukewarm water	50 mL
2 tbsp	dry yeast	30 mL
3 cups	flour (approximately)	750 mL
3/4 cup	oatmeal	175 mL
2 tbsp	butter	30 mL
2 tsp	salt	10 mL
1 cup	water (approximately)	250 mL

Stir molasses into warm water. Sprinkle with yeast. Cover and let rest 10 minutes while yeast proofs.

Meanwhile place flour, butter and salt in a food processor. Process in on-off bursts until just mixed.

When yeast has foamed, add to flour mixture through the feed tube with the processor running. Add remaining water in a slow stream, processing only until dough forms a ball and cleans the side of the bowl. (A drop more water may be necessary.)

Turn dough into an oiled bowl. Turn dough over to oil the top, cover the dish and let sit in a warm place until doubled. Punch dough down, form into a loaf, and place in a greased 9 inch (2 L) loaf pan. Let rise again until it has topped the pan.

Preheat oven to 400 F (200 C). Bake loaf 15 minutes. Reduce heat to 375 F (190 C) and bake 40 minutes, or until crust is a deep golden brown and sounds hollow when thumped. Serve hot with lots of butter. Makes 1 loaf.

Oatmeal Bread

A slice of still-warm oatmeal bread with butter melting into it is one of life's true pleasures.

1 3/4 cups	water	425 mL
1/4 cup	butter	50 mL
1/4 cup	molasses	50 mL
4 cups	flour (approximately)	1 L
1 1/2 cups	uncooked oatmeal	375 mL
1/2 cup	sunflower seeds	125 mL
2	eggs	2
2	pkgs dry yeast	2
1 tbsp	salt	15 mL
	egg wash made of 1 egg white beaten with 1 tbsp (15 mL) water	

Heat water, butter and molasses together to 120 F (45 C). In a large bowl, combine 2 cups (500 mL) flour with oats, sunflower seeds, eggs, yeast, salt and warm water mixture, stirring to make a soft dough. Beat dough 5 minutes.

Stir in remaining flour. Turn out onto a floured surface and knead to a moderately stiff dough, adding a little additional flour if dough seems sticky. (The amount of flour will depend on the amount of humidity in the air.) Place dough in a greased bowl and let rise in a warm place until doubled in bulk, about 1 hour.

Punch down and divide into 2 equal parts. Form into loaves. Place each in a greased 9 inch (2 L) loaf pan. Let rise again until doubled in bulk. Brush loaves with egg wash. Bake at 375 F (190 C) about 40 minutes, or until done. Remove from pans and cool on a rack. Makes 2 loaves.

Cinnamon Stickies

For the bun lover, these cinnamon stickies are quite possibly the ultimate, having both a topping and a filling. There's no finer way to spoil yourself than with warm cinnamon buns and a pot of good coffee.

TOPPING

1/2 cup	brown sugar, firmly packed	125 mL
1/2 cup	margarine, softened	125 mL
2 tbsp	light corn syrup	30 mL

Preheat oven to 375 F (190 C). Butter a 9 x 13 inch (3 L) pan. In a small bowl, combine ingredients and blend well. Spread evenly in prepared pan. Set aside.

ROLLS

3 to 3 1/2 cups	all-purpose flour	750 to 875 mL
1/4 cup	sugar	50 mL
1 tsp	salt	5 mL
1	pkg active dry yeast (quick rise)	1
1 cup	water	250 mL
2 tbsp	margarine or butter	30 mL
1	egg	1

In a large bowl, combine 1 1/2 cups (375 mL) flour, sugar, salt and yeast. Blend well. In a small saucepan, heat water and margarine until very warm, about 130 F (50 C).

Add warm liquid and egg to flour mixture. Blend at low speed until moistened and then beat 3 minutes at medium speed. Stir in 1 1/2 to 2 cups (375 to 500 mL) flour until dough pulls cleanly away from sides of bowl. On a floured surface, knead 1 minute. Roll dough into a 9 x 5 inch (22 x 12 cm) rectangle.

FILLING

3 tbsp	margarine, softened	45 mL
1/2 cup	brown sugar	125 mL
2 tsp	cinnamon	10 mL

Spread 2 tbsp (30 mL) margarine over dough. Combine sugar and cinnamon. Sprinkle over margarine. Starting with 5 inch (12 cm) side, roll up tightly, pressing edges to seal.

Cut into 12 slices. Place cut-side-down in the prepared pan. Cover loosely with a plastic wrap and cloth towel. Let rise in a warm place until light and doubled in size, about 35 to 45 minutes. Bake 25 to 30 minutes or until golden brown. Cool briefly, about 1 minute, then turn onto a serving platter. Makes 1 dozen rolls.

Onion Twists

On the weekend when you decide to relax and make a pot of homemade soup from scratch, or maybe a pot of beans, do yourself a favor and bake these yeasty onion twists.

1	pkg active dry yeast	1
1 cup	lukewarm water	250 mL
2 tsp	sugar	10 mL
1 tsp	salt	5 mL
3 cups	flour, sifted (approximately)	750 mL
3 tbsp	butter	45 mL
1	large onion, chopped	1
3 tbsp	butter, melted	45 mL
	paprika	

In a large bowl dissolve yeast in water. Add sugar, salt and 1 1/2 cups (375 mL) flour. Using a mixer at medium speed, beat 2 minutes.

Stir in enough remaining flour to make a soft dough. Turn out onto a lightly floured surface. Knead about 5 minutes, or until smooth and elastic. If dough is sticky, add up to 1/4 cup (50 mL) more flour.

Place in a large greased bowl, turning dough over so that top is greased. Cover with a towel and let rise in a warm place until doubled, about 1 hour.

Meanwhile melt 3 tbsp (45 mL) butter in a frypan. Add onion and cook until tender, but not brown. Remove from heat and set aside.

Punch down dough. Cover and let rest 10 minutes.

On a lightly floured surface roll dough into a 16 x 12 inch (40 x 30 cm) rectangle. Spread 1/2 onions in a 3 inch (7 cm) strip lengthwise down center of dough. Fold 1/3 dough over onions. Spread remaining onions on top, then fold remaining 1/3 of dough. Pat gently to flatten.

Cut dough crosswise into 16 strips. Twist each strip twice and place strips 2 inches (5 cm) apart on a greased large baking sheet.

Cover and let rise until doubled, about 30 minutes. Brush twists with 1/2 melted butter. Sprinkle with paprika.

Bake in a 375 F (190 C) oven 25 minutes, or until golden brown. Brush with remaining melted butter. Serve warm. Makes 16 twists.

Basic Pizza Dough

Here's a basic, easy-to-make, tender pizza dough. It can be rolled thin and baked at a high temperature for a crisp crust, as it is in Italy, or rolled thick and baked longer at a lower temperature for a softer, bread-like crust. This recipe makes one huge cookie-sheet pizza or a couple of smaller round ones.

DOUGH

3 tbsp	lukewarm water	45 mL
1	pkg fast-rising yeast	1
3 cups	all-purpose flour (approximately)	750 mL
1 tsp	salt	5 mL
1 tbsp	butter, melted	15 mL
1 cup	milk	250 mL

Stir together water, yeast and 1 tbsp (15 mL) flour. Let rest in a warm place until it foams.

Stir in 1/2 flour with salt, melted butter and milk. Work in remaining flour. (The dough will require more or less flour, depending on the amount of moisture in the air.) Turn onto a well-floured board and knead until smooth and elastic.

Let rise in a warm place until doubled in bulk, about 1 hour.

Punch dough down and roll on a well-floured board. The pizza need not be round–any shape will do as long as it fits the pan reasonably well. Drape dough over rolling pin and ease onto a well-oiled pan. (If using baking tiles, scatter them with cornmeal.) Press dough into a flattened shape. Dress and bake at 450 F (230 C) about 20 to 25 minutes for a thin crust, 30 minutes at 375 degrees F (190 C) for a thick crust. Let cool slightly before cutting. Makes 1 large pizza.

GARNISHES

Use as much or as little as you like.

Mozzarella, chopped tomatoes and black olives
Parmesan, sliced mushrooms and red onions
Mozzarella, prosciutto and chopped tomatoes
Mozzarella, pepperoni, green peppers and tomato sauce
Goat cheese, sun-dried tomatoes and red onions
Brie, smoked salmon and green onion
Mozzarella, barbecued chicken and tomato salsa

Two-Cheese Calzone with Sun-Dried Tomatoes

Calzone is the perfect walk-away meal. I first ate it years ago on Italian trains, where it's sold through the windows during station stops. Our burgeoning Italian population has since introduced it to a lot of grateful people.

1	recipe Basic Pizza Dough	1
1 cup	mozzarella, grated	250 mL
1/2 cup	feta or goat cheese, crumbled	125 mL
1	green onion, chopped	1
1/4 cup	sun-dried tomatoes, chopped	50 ml
1 tbsp	olive oil	15 mL
2 tsp	herbs of your choice	10 mL

Preheat oven to 450 F (230 C). Place rack at lowest position in the oven. Roll and stretch dough until slightly oval.

Mix mozzarella, feta, green onion, sun-dried tomatoes and herbs, and spread mixture over 1/2 dough. Fold dough over like a turnover and pinch to seal. Place on an oiled baking sheet.

Bake until barely browned, about 10 minutes. Brush with oil and return to the oven until golden brown and slightly puffed. Cool a few minutes before slicing. Serves 2 generously.

Focaccia

Although focaccia is often made with onions, it doesn't usually contain cheese. But Anna Cinari, a Ligurian friend who interpreted for me during a trip to Italy, makes it this way and it's delicious. As far as I know, it's also unique to Anna's kitchen. Parmesan cheese or even Romano may be used in place of Pecorino.

1	medium yellow onion, chopped	1
1	clove garlic, minced	1
1	recipe Basic Dizza Dough	1
1 tbsp	olive oil	15 mL
1 cup	Pecorino cheese, grated	250 mL
1 tsp	basil	5 mL
	rosemary, olive oil and coarse salt to taste	

Preheat oven to 450 F (230 C).

Fry onion and garlic. Cool.

Flatten pizza dough with your hands and pat into a rectangle. Sprinkle fried onions, cheese and basil over top. Fold 1/3 dough toward middle. Fold other side also toward middle, covering first side. (Dough will now be 1/3 its original width.) Pat again firmly to flatten. Shape as you please, leaving dough about 1/2 inch (1 cm) thick. With your fingers make definite dents all over dough. Drizzle with good olive oil and sprinkle with rosemary and coarse salt. Bake until golden brown, about 25 minutes.

Most Italians buy their focaccia in neat squares from a baker, but Anna serves hers whole, straight from the oven, and everyone tears off a chunk. Serves 6 to 8.

Stuffed Pizza Zenari

In some parts of Italy, pizza is stuffed, filled, covered with more dough and baked much like a pie. Adriano Zenari's personal version of stuffed pizza takes as much or as little filling as you wish. Amounts given are approximate.

If speed is of the essence, use a large packaged pizza mix.

1	recipe Basic Pizza Dough	1
	olive oil	
	basil and oregano to taste	
1	onion, finely chopped	1
1	green pepper, thinly sliced	1
handful	mushrooms, sliced	handful
1 cup	mozzarella, grated	250 mL
6 oz	Black Forest ham, thinly sliced	180 g
1/2 cup	pesto	125 mL
1 tbsp	extra virgin olive oil	15 mL
2 or 3	fresh plum tomatoes, thinly sliced	2 or 3
	additional mozzarella to taste	
	Parmesan cheese	

Make your favorite recipe for pizza dough. Roll out 2/3 dough and cover sides and bottom of a deep dish pizza pan, letting some dough hang over edge to seal top.

Brush interior with olive oil and sprinkle with basil and oregano. Add onion, green peppers and mushrooms. Sprinkle with mozzarella cheese. Add a layer of Black Forest ham.

Roll out remaining 1/3 dough and place on top of pizza. Pinch edges together as you would a pie crust. Cut slits in top of dough to allow steam to escape during baking. Brush top with a mixture of pesto and oil.

Add a layer of tomatoes. Cover generously with mozzarella. Sprinkle with Parmesan.

Bake at 350 F (180 C) about 30 to 45 minutes, until cheese is bubbly and crust is golden. Serve with olives, raw sweet peppers and red wine. Serves 8 as an appetizer, serves 4 as a main course with olives.

Note: Small jars of pesto are available in Italian grocery stores and good delis.

Green Chili Spoon Bread

Spoon bread is soft, comforting, almost pillowy in the mouth. This one came from a California chef who got it from his Polish grandma–further proof that food is the international language.

3/4 cup	cornmeal	175 mL
1 1/2 cups	cold water	375 mL
4 tbsp	butter, softened	60 mL
2 cups	Cheddar cheese, grated	500 mL
1 tsp	salt	5 mL
1 cup	milk	250 mL
4	egg yolks, beaten	4
1/2 cup	canned green chilis, chopped	125 mL
1/2 cup	pitted black olives, sliced	125 mL
4	egg whites, beaten stiff	4

Preheat oven to 325 F (160 C).

Stir cornmeal into cold water in a saucepan and cook, stirring constantly, until mixture boils and thickens. Remove from heat.

Add butter, cheese and salt to cornmeal mixture. Combine milk and egg yolks and stir into cornmeal mixture. Add chili peppers and olives. Stir to combine.

Fold egg whites into mixture and pour into a large, buttered cast iron frypan or an oven-proof casserole. Smooth the top. Bake 50 to 60 minutes. Serves 4 to 6.

Olive Onion Biscuit Bread

Here's an easy quick-bread to serve warm with scrambled eggs. Add a basket of fresh vegetables–radishes, green onions, carrot sticks–and you've got lunch.

2 cups	biscuit mix	500 mL
2 tbsp	fresh parsley, chopped	30 mL
2/3 cup	cold water	150 mL
1	large onion, diced	1
2 tbsp	butter	30 mL
1/2 cup	sour cream or yogurt	125 mL
1	egg, beaten	1
1 tsp	dried dillweed	5 mL
3/4 cup	olives, chopped	175 mL
	salt and pepper to taste	

Preheat oven to 450 F (230 C). Combine biscuit mix, parsley and cold water. Spoon into a greased 9 inch (2 L) pan.

Sauté onions in butter until golden brown. Season lightly with salt and pepper. Combine sour cream (or yogurt), egg, dillweed and olives. Add onions and mix. Spoon over bread.

Bake 20 minutes. Let cool in the pan 10 minutes before slicing. Serves 4 to 6.

Fiesta Bread

Any time you need a casual snack, think fiesta bread.

2 cups	ripe tomatoes, chopped	500 mL
1	clove garlic, minced	1
2	green onions, chopped	2
1/4 cup	black olives, sliced	50 mL
1/2 tsp	dried oregano	2 mL
1	large loaf French bread	1
2 cups	Monterey Jack cheese, grated	500 mL
1/4 cup	Parmesan cheese, grated	50 mL

Preheat oven to 425 F (220 C). Combine tomatoes, garlic, green onion, olives and oregano. Cut bread in half lengthwise. Sprinkle halves with cheese. Spoon on tomato mixture and sprinkle with Parmesan. Bake 10 minutes. Serves 6 to 8.

Cheesy Bacon Squares

This recipe came to us from the Pillsbury people, who have been the inspiration for a number of my Fast Track Menus. Although it's designed as a nibble to serve with drinks, it makes a nice light lunch with a salad.

11 oz	tube soft breadsticks	311 g
1/2 lb	bacon, chopped, cooked and drained	250 g
4	eggs	4
1/2 cup	milk	125 mL
2 cups	Cheddar cheese, grated	500 mL
1	green onion, chopped	1
1/2 tsp	dry mustard	2 mL
	salt and pepper to taste	
dash	each, Worcestershire and Tabasco sauce	dash
2 tbsp	Parmesan cheese, grated	30 mL

Preheat oven to 350 F (180 C). Unroll breadstick dough and press into an ungreased 9 x 13 inch (3 L) pan. Press over bottom and 1/2 inch (1 cm) up side to form crust. Bake 15 minutes and remove from oven.

Meanwhile, in a small bowl, whisk together bacon, eggs, milk, Cheddar, green onion and seasonings. Pour egg mixture over partially baked crust and sprinkle with Parmesan. Bake an additional 20 to 25 minutes, or until filling sets in center. Let cool 5 minutes before carefully removing to a cutting board. Serve warm or cold. Cut into 24 squares.

Crunchy Mexican Sticks

Super-fast breadsticks to serve with a good bowl of soup on a cold November night.

1/2 cup	tortilla chips, crushed	125 mL
2 tbsp	Parmesan cheese, grated	30 mL
11 oz	tube soft breadsticks	311 g
1 cup	taco sauce	250 ml

Heat oven to 350 F (180 C). In a small pie plate, combine crushed tortilla chips and Parmesan. Unroll breadstick dough. Cut across dough horizontally and separate into 16 short breadsticks. Brush dough liberally with taco sauce. Roll breadsticks in cheese mixture to coat. Twist each breadstick. Place on an ungreased cookie sheet, pressing ends down firmly. Bake 15 to 20 minutes. Serve warm. Makes 16 sticks.

FAST TRACK MENU

Speedy Deep Pizza
Pears in Maple Syrup

Speedy Deep Pizza

Grandma may not have approved, but when you fall through the door at 6 pm with a hungry family getting grumpier by the minute, refrigerated doughs are a lifesaver.

1 1/2 lb	ground beef	750 g
1	medium onion, chopped	1
7 1/2 oz	can pizza sauce	213 mL
2 tbsp	Parmesan cheese, grated	30 mL
1 tsp	oregano	5 mL
	salt and pepper to taste	
8 oz	can refrigerated biscuits	227 g
1 cup	mushrooms, sliced	250 mL
1	tomato, sliced	1
1 cup	mozzarella cheese, grated	250 mL
	green pepper rings	
3 to 4	pitted black olives, sliced (optional)	3 to 4

Preheat oven to 350 F (180 C). Grease a 9 inch (22 cm) pie pan. Brown ground beef and onion. Drain. Stir in pizza sauce, 1 tbsp (15 mL) Parmesan, oregano, salt and pepper. Simmer while preparing crust.

Separate dough into 10 biscuits. Arrange biscuits in the prepared pan. Press over bottom and up sides to form crust. Spoon hot meat mixture onto crust. Arrange mushroom and tomato slices over meat and top with mozzarella. Arrange green pepper rings and olives, if desired, over cheese and sprinkle with remaining Parmesan cheese. Bake 20 to 25 minutes, or until crust is deep golden brown. Cool 5 minutes before serving. Serves 4.

Pears in Maple Syrup

4	pears	4
1 cup	maple syrup	250 mL
1 cup	whipping cream	250 mL
1/2 cup	plain yogurt	125 mL
4 tsp	butter	20 mL

Core pears from blossom end. Do not peel. Rub pears with butter. Place in a shallow baking dish. Pour syrup around pears. Bake at 400 F (200 C) 20 minutes, or until syrup is bubbling. Baste pears once or twice with juices. Bake another 10 minutes.

Whip cream, fold in yogurt and spoon over hot pears. Serves 4.

CHAPTER 12
December

The Merriest Month

December Recipes

Now comes the time of reckoning. It's Christmas, and as usual I won't find the perfect gift for everybody on my list, won't get my cards mailed on time, won't get the pudding made or the turkey smoked or the dog groomed, even though every other dog in the neighborhood is sporting red ribbons.

But consider. Is this a time to wallow in my own shortcomings? The world still turns without my pudding. My unkempt dog still loves me.

Now is the time to gather around our own tables and enjoy. And let's establish one thing right away: try as we might, we cannot have a just little bit of Christmas. There is no such thing as *Noel Minceur*.

So, sometime in December, have a party. One is enough if it's terrific. (Refuse to be intimidated by socialites waving full calendars. There's no law that says you must entertain the entire town or even the street.) Go for quality in friends, food and drink.

Make it a family party. DO involve the children.

"Fluffie dear, you're a big girl now, so stop snivelling and start whacking up those onions. Mommy needs them to stuff the goose." The child will feel wise and useful, and it's one less thing for you to do.

If people drop in unexpectedly or they're a tad early for your party, invite them into the kitchen and let them help.

"No, Portia, of COURSE you're not too early! You're just in time to pluck the geese. We have three this year."

Some guests will come and stay. And stay. When they ask what they can bring (and they will), don't be shy about telling them.

"Portia, how sweet of you to ask. We could use a turkey. A nice 25 pounder should do it, and would you have it smoked?" (Portia was about to volunteer for pickles. She'll be wiser next year.)

Throughout the season play wonderful music, all the things you love, whenever you feel like it. Fill the house with sweet-smelling spruce trimmings; most tree lots will sell you an armload for a dollar if you pick them up while you're buying the tree. Boil cinnamon sticks. Toss tangerine peels in the fireplace. When planning party menus, keep them simple but wonderful. If you serve a casserole, a salad and an easy bread, knock them out with three desserts, all chocolate.

Sleep in once. Drink champagne. Read some Dickens. Sing a carol. Roll on, Christmas!

Hot Cider

December is the time for sudden blizzards and for being storm-stuck with no way home until morning. Should the need arise to comfort many people at once, serve this heart-warming cider.

9	whole cloves	9
1	whole allspice	1
4	2 inch (1 cm) pieces stick cinnamon, broken	4
4 qt	apple cider	4 L
1 cup	brown sugar, firmly packed	250 mL
2	lemons, thinly sliced	2

Tie cloves, allspice and cinnamon in a cheesecloth. Place in a large kettle with cider and sugar. Simmer 5 minutes. Just before serving, remove spice bag. Serve in mugs with lemon afloat. Enough for 8 to 12, depending on how thirsty your guests are.

Irish Cream

One of my most reuqested recipes, this came from an unknown source. But I'm grateful to you, whoever you are.

1 cup	whipping cream	250 mL
3	eggs	3
1 cup	Irish whisky	250 mL
1/4 tsp	coconut flavoring	1 mL
1 1/4 cups	sweetened condensed milk	300 mL

Combine all ingredients in a blender. Serve immediately or store, refrigerated, for up to 1 week. (It'll never last that long.) Makes 3 cups.

Pastry-Wrapped Brie with Blue Cheese

No matter how many *hors d'oeuvres* you might slave over, this easy pastry-wrapped brie is sure to be a winner. Don't be put off by the unusual combination of blue cheese and apricot jam–it's delicious.

10 oz	brie cheese wheel	315 g
1/2 cup	blue cheese, crumbled	125 mL
1/4 cup	apricot jam	50 mL
1/2 cup	almonds, sliced	125 mL
1	egg, beaten	1
	pastry for a single-crust pie	

Preheat oven to 350 F (180 C). Slice brie in half horizontally and sprinkle blue cheese on bottom half, making sure rind is on outside. Replace top half of brie. Spread top with apricot jam and sprinkle with almonds.

Wrap brie in pastry, folding ends underneath brie wheel and trimming excess so it doesn't get too thick. Decorate top with pastry scraps if you wish. Brush pastry with egg. Chill 20 minutes.

Place pastry-wrapped brie on a cookie sheet and bake 30 minutes, or until golden. Serves 4 as an appetizer.

Marinated Chicken Strips

I got this recipe from a journalist friend who went to France on a holiday and decided to stay. Now he's studying at Ferrandi, hoping to become a chef.

4	boneless, skinless chicken breasts	4
1 cup	dry white wine	250 ml
2	cloves garlic, minced	2
	juice of 2 lemons	
1/3 cup	green onions, thinly sliced	75 mL
2 tbsp	dried tarragon	30 mL
2 to 3 tbsp	olive oil	30 to 45 mL
	salt and pepper to taste	
	sesame seeds	

Cut chicken into thin strips and combine with wine in a saucepan. Cover and gently poach chicken over low heat until tender, about 15 minutes.

Place chicken and wine in a large bowl, then stir in all remaining ingredients except sesame seeds. Cover and chill overnight.

Drain before serving and sprinkle with sesame seeds. Serves 6 to 8.

Hot Artichoke Cheese Dip

This sounds a little strange, but is devilishly easy and just the thing for a busy season.

14 oz	jar marinated artichoke hearts	440 g
1/2 cup	green chilies, seeded and chopped	125 mL
4	jalapeño chilies, seeded and finely chopped	4
6 tbsp	mayonnaise	90 mL
2 cups	sharp Cheddar cheese, grated	500 mL

Drain and chop artichokes, and spread on a greased shallow baking dish. Sprinkle chilies over artichokes and spread mayonnaise over entire mixture. Top with cheese and bake at 350 F (180 C) 15 minutes, or until cheese melts.

Serve hot with tortilla or corn chips. Makes 2 1/2 cups (625 mL).

Note: This dip can be made a day in advance and refrigerated before being baked. Bake as above until cheese melts and dip is hot.

Crunchy Spinach Dip in Mini Pitas

A good dip for armchair quarterbacks.

10 oz	pkg frozen spinach, thawed, well-drained and chopped	284 g
1 cup	mayonnaise	250 mL
1 cup	sour cream	250 mL
1	large red onion, chopped	1
1 cup	water chestnuts	250 mL
3 oz	pkg Knorr's vegetable soup mix	85 g
12	mini pitas	12

Blend all ingredients well. Chill. At serving time, cut pitas in half to form a pocket. Spoon 1 tbsp (15 mL) filling into pita pockets. Makes 24.

Lentil Mushroom Soup

On a cold night, a bowl of lentil soup with nuggets of mushrooms will warm the cockles of your heart. A good choice for a casual party.

3 cups	onions, chopped	750 mL
2	stalks celery, diced	2
1 1/2 lb	mushrooms, coarsely chopped	750 g
3	garlic cloves, minced	3
2 tbsp	olive oil	30 mL
1 lb	lentils, rinsed and drained	500 g
3 qt	water	3 L
3 tbsp	lemon juice	45 mL
1 tsp	paprika	15 mL
	salt to taste	
	sour cream and chives for garnish	

Sauté onion, celery, mushrooms and garlic in olive oil 5 minutes, or until softened. Stir in lentils; sauté 1 minute. Add water, bring to boil and reduce to simmer. Cook, uncovered, over medium heat until lentils are very soft and soup has thickened, about 45 minutes. Stir in lemon juice, paprika and salt. Serve garnished with sour cream and chives. Serves 8.

Favorite Stuffing

This stuffing is food writer Gordon Morash's favorite.

"In our house, the stuffing is always the first Christmas food item to go, so we arm ourselves with two batches. I use various kinds of sausages, sometimes apples and raisins. The bread mix can include egg bread, bagels, hot dog or hamburger buns, wholegrain bread or even plain old white. I cook this more conventional stuffing outside the turkey and save a bit of time on roasting."

1 lb	pork sausage meat	500 g
2	onions, finely chopped	2
3	stalks celery with leaves, chopped	3
1/4 cup	butter (optional)	50 mL
3 tsp	poultry seasoning or sage	15 mL
1 tsp	salt	5 mL
1/2 tsp	pepper	2 mL
3 tbsp	fresh parsley, chopped	45 mL
12 to 15 cups	stale bread cubes	3 to 3.75 L
2 cups	chicken or turkey broth (to moisten)	500 mL

Fry sausage meat until brown, breaking up with a fork. Remove to a bowl using a slotted spoon. Cook onions and celery until tender in remaining fat and butter. Combine meat and vegetables with seasonings and bread, adding enough broth to moisten. If stuffing turkey, fill both cavities loosely. This quantity is enough for a 20 lb (9 kg) bird.

If cooking stuffing outside turkey, place in an electric frypan on low. Cook, covered, 40 to 60 minutes. Stir occasionally to ensure stuffing is not drying out or burning. Add more stock as necessary.

Stuffing may also be cooked, covered, in a buttered casserole for the last hour of turkey's roasting. Stir occasionally and add stock if stuffing dries. Serves 8 to 10.

Ayrshire Shortbread

Doug Skinner is a true Scot. Here he is, being eloquent about one of his favorite cookies.

"You can tell it's Christmas when the tartan boxes appear. They're stacked on the ends of the aisles in the Foods From Britain section. The boxes contain Scotland's great contribution to Yule festivities: Shortbread.

"And the marketers insist on imprinting the cakes with 'Frae Bonnie Scotland', 'A Guid New Year Tae Ane and A' and other such-like sickeners.

"But even when it's The Right Stuff, buttery and message-free, those boxes are a waste of good money. Shortbread is easy, costs little and takes little time to make."

Here's his version.

1/2 cup	flour	125 mL
1/2 cup	rice flour	125 mL
1/2 cup	butter	125 mL
1/2 cup	berry sugar	125 mL
1	egg yolk	1
3/4 cup	cream	175 mL

Sieve flour and rice flour together. Rub in butter with your fingertips. Add sugar and bind mixture to a stiff consistency with egg yolk and cream.

Roll out thinly, prick with a fork and cut into desired shapes. Place on wax paper on a cookie sheet and bake about 15 minutes, until golden brown, at 325 F (160 C). Cool. Makes about 2 dozen cookies.

Christmas Cake

Linda Hughes, a working mother, has fond memories of her childhood Christmases. "This is Nana's cake. She made it every year, and now I make it, with 2 pounds of currants instead of Nana's 3."

10	eggs	10
1 lb	butter	500 g
4 cups	flour	1 L
1 lb	berry sugar	500 g
2 lb	currants	1 kg
1/2 lb	glacé cherries	250 g
1 lb	mixed peel	500 g
1/2 lb	almonds	250 g
1 cup	brandy	250 mL

Chop cherries and nuts, and mix with currants and peel in a large bowl. Add flour and mix until well coated.

In a separate bowl, cream butter. Add eggs and sugar and mix well.

Combine all ingredients, stirring in brandy gradually. Pour into 2 large loaf pans lined with greased brown paper. Put in a 350 F (180 C) oven 30 minutes. Reduce heat to 325 F (160 C) and continue baking 30 minutes to 1 hour longer, until top is brown and cracked. Makes 2 loaves.

Cinnamon Loaf

Donna Woronuik offers this Christmas favorite.

"This has been a family favorite for years and has been passed on to many relatives and friends. It's good made with sour milk, but better with buttermilk. I've never had a flop, even when I double the recipe, which is most of the time."

LOAF

1/4 cup	butter or margarine	50 mL
1 cup	white sugar	250 mL
2	eggs	2
2 cups	flour	500 mL
pinch	salt	pinch
1 tsp	baking powder	5 mL
1/2 tsp	baking soda	2 mL
1 cup	sour milk or buttermilk	250 mL
2 tsp	vanilla	10 mL

TOPPING

3 tbsp	brown sugar	45 mL
1 tbsp	cinnamon	15 mL

Preheat oven to 350 F (180 C). Grease a 9 inch (2 L) loaf pan, line with wax paper and then grease again.

Cream butter with sugar and add vanilla. Beat in eggs. Combine dry ingredients and add alternately with milk.

Pour 1/2 batter into the prepared loaf pan. Sprinkle with 1/2 topping, pour in remaining batter and cover with remaining topping. Run a knife criss-cross through batter. Bake 1 hour. Makes 1 loaf.

Pear Mincemeat

When I first saw this recipe, I put it aside because it would take more time than I usually had. Then a friend made me a batch, and I ate it on the spot. It's even better over ice cream. Scrumptious, and worth the trouble.

1 cup	currants	250 ml
1 cup	sultana raisins	250 mL
1/2 cup	dried apricots, coarsely chopped	125 mL
	juice and grated rind of 1 lemon	
	juice and grated rind of 1 orange	
1/2 cup	brown sugar, lightly packed	125 mL
2 tsp	ground cinnamon	10 mL
2 tsp	ground nutmeg	10 mL
1/2 tsp	ground ginger	2 mL
pinch	pickling salt	pinch
10	large pears	10
1 cup	slivered blanched almonds	250 mL
1/4 cup	rum	50 mL

In a large stainless steel or enamel pan, combine all ingredients except pears, almonds and rum.

Peel, core and chop pears. Stir into fruit mixture. Bring to boil, reduce heat, cover and simmer 30 minutes, stirring occasionally.

Lower heat under fruit mixture and continue cooking uncovered, stirring occasionally until very thick, about 15 minutes. Stir in almonds and rum, and simmer 5 minutes longer.

Fill a canner with water. Place 5 individual 1/2 qt (500 mL) jars with lids in canner over high heat. Boil 5 minutes.

Ladle mincemeat into hot jars to within 1/2 inch (1 cm) of top rim. Seal and place jars in canner.

Cover canner and return water to boil. Process 20 minutes. Cool 24 hours. Label and store in a cool dark place. Makes 5 full 1/2 qt (500 mL) jars.

Butter Tart Squares

Marilyn Moysa parted with a real winner with this recipe.

"This is my mother's and my favorite at Christmas. She was a great cook and anyone who knew her will know this is delicious."

SQUARES

1 1/4 cups	flour	300 mL
1/2 cup	butter or margarine	125 mL
1/4 cup	brown sugar	50 mL

Preheat oven to 350 F (180 C). Place together in a food processor or blender. Whir about 3 times until butter is mixed. Pat into a 9 inch (22 cm) square pan. Bake 15 minutes. Cool slightly.

TOPPING

1 cup	brown sugar	250 mL
1/3 cup	butter	75 mL
1	egg	1
2 tbsp	cream	30 mL
1 tbsp	flour	15 mL
1 cup	currants **OR**	250 mL
1/2 cup	currants **AND**	125 mL
1/2 cup	pecans, chopped	125 mL

Beat together brown sugar, butter, egg and cream.

Mix flour with currants or currant-pecan combination. Spread mixture over base and bake 30 to 35 minutes. Freezes well. Serves 12.

Spiced Walnuts

If you're a nibbler, you'll find these irresistible. They also make a nice gift. To be sure the walnut pieces are fresh, buy whole walnuts and crack your own.

2 tbsp	butter	30 mL
4 cups	walnut pieces	1 L
2 tbsp	curry powder	30 mL
1 tbsp	ground cumin	15 mL
l tsp	salt	5 mL
1/2 tsp	sugar	2 mL

In a large skillet, melt butter over medium heat. Add walnuts and sauté 3 to 4 minutes, tossing often. Stir in curry, cumin, salt and sugar. Sauté, tossing often, 2 to 3 minutes. Cool, then store in an airtight container at room temperature for up to 2 weeks. Makes 4 cups (1 L).

Rum Balls

These are veteran candymaker Bill McCreedy's favorite sweet.

2 cups	semisweet chocolate chips	500 mL
1 1/2 cups	sweetened condensed milk	375 mL
1/4 cup	dark rum	50 mL
	ground pecans	

In a heavy saucepan over low heat, melt chocolate chips with sweetened condensed milk. Remove from heat and stir in rum. Chill 2 to 3 hours. Roll into 1/2 inch (1 cm) balls and roll in ground pecans. Makes about 72.

FAST TRACK MENU

Day-After Turkey
No-Name Num-Nums
Turnips Again
Mincemeat Cake

Day-After Turkey

1/2 cup	green pepper, diced	125 mL
1	stalk celery	1
2	green onions, chopped	2
2 tbsp	butter	30 mL
10 oz	can cream of mushroom soup	284 mL
1/2 cup	salad dressing	125 mL
1/4 cup	milk	50 mL
2 cups	cooked rice	500 mL
2 cups	turkey, diced	500 mL

Preheat oven to 350 F (180 C).

Fry pepper, celery and onion in butter. In a 1 qt (1 L) casserole dish, blend soup, salad dressing and milk, and fold into remaining ingredients. Bake 35 minutes. Serves 4 to 6.

No-Name Num-Nums

2 cups	canned water chestnuts	500 mL
	dark soya sauce to cover	
1/4 cup	brown sugar	50 mL
8 slices	side bacon, halved	8 slices

Marinate water chestnuts overnight in dark soya sauce. Roll nuts in brown sugar, then wrap in side bacon, securing with a toothpick. Grill until bacon is crisp. Serve hot. Serves 4 to 6.

Turnips Again

Leftover turnips? They're better this way than in their original form.

3 cups	cooked turnips, mashed	750 mL
2 tbsp	butter	30 mL
2	eggs	2
3 tbsp	flour	45 mL
1 tbsp	brown sugar	15 mL
1 tsp	baking powder	5 mL
1/2 tsp	salt	2 mL
1/4 tsp	pepper	1 mL
1/2 cup	bread crumbs, buttered	125 mL

Preheat oven to 375 F (190 C). Combine turnip with butter. Beat eggs, then add flour, sugar, baking powder, salt and pepper. Combine turnips with egg mixture, turn into a 2 qt (2 L) greased casserole pan. Top with buttered bread crumbs. Bake about 30 minutes. Serves 4 to 6 generously.

Mincemeat Cake

My father's solution to unexpected company.

1 1/4 cups	flour	300 mL
1 1/4 cups	quick rolled oats	300 mL
3/4 cup	brown sugar	175 mL
1 cup	butter	250 mL
2 cups	mincemeat	500 mL

Preheat oven to 350 F (180 C). Put flour, rolled oats and sugar in a bowl. Cut in butter. Press 1/2 mixture into a 9 inch (22 cm) pan.

Spread mincemeat over crumb base. Sprinkle with remaining crumbs and press down firmly. Bake about 30 minutes. Makes 1 cake.

Index

ENTRÉES

SALADS